SIR THO

URNE

THE GARDEN OF CYRUS

SIR THOMAS BROWNE

URNE BURIALL

AND

THE GARDEN OF CYRUS

EDITED BY
JOHN CARTER

CAMBRIDGE
AT THE UNIVERSITY PRESS
1967

CAMBRIDGE
UNIVERSITY PRESS

University Printing House, Cambridge CB2 8BS, United Kingdom

Cambridge University Press is part of the University of Cambridge.

It furthers the University's mission by disseminating knowledge in the pursuit of
education, learning and research at the highest international levels of excellence.

www.cambridge.org
Information on this title: www.cambridge.org/9781316606865

© Cambridge University Press 1967

First published 1958
Reprinted 1967
First paperback edition 2016

A catalogue record for this publication is available from the British Library

ISBN 978-0-521-04351-9 Hardback
ISBN 978-1-316-60686-5 Paperback

CONTENTS

PREFACE

IT is three hundred years since the publication, by Henry Brome, at the Sign of the Gun in Ivy Lane, of a rather shoddily printed small octavo volume containing two of the most precious glories of English prose.

The author, Thomas Browne, Doctor of Physic, as he styled himself on the title-page, was then fifty-five years of age. He had already published, fifteen years earlier, *Religio Medici*, the work of philosophical reflection for which he is chiefly remembered today, and, in 1646, *Pseudodoxia Epidemica* (commonly known as 'Browne's Vulgar Errors'), the collection of scientific and historical speculations which was even more widely popular during his own lifetime. In 1716, thirty-four years after its author's death and without benefit of his final revision, was published *Christian Morals*, that essay which to Lytton Strachey seemed almost like an elaborate and magnificent parody of the Book of Proverbs and which so powerfully influenced the prose style of Dr Johnson.

Urne Buriall and *The Garden of Cyrus*, the two 'wonderful deliverances' which George Saintsbury considered to contain 'the quintessence both of Browne's thought and of his expression', were the perfected products of his maturity. Their factual contents, like their ostensible occasions, are antiquarian and 'scientific' in the unscientific manner of that omnivorously inquiring age: indeed, some passages in both the essays read like extracts from a very unusual kind of notebook, constantly illuminated by a flashing or fantastic phrase. But for the most part, and particularly in *Urne Buriall*, the curious lore, the strange fantasies, the whimsical speculations, the extraordinary conceits, the relish for picturesque legend and equally picturesque reality, the fascination exerted on the author by bizarre historical and mythical figures—all these jewelled elements, like the thousand small pieces of stained glass in a great rose window, are harmonised by Browne's deeply reflective imagination, and patterned, with the most polished and elaborate artistry, into paragraph after paragraph of baroque magnificence.

However, where Johnson and Coleridge, Pater and Saintsbury, and (perhaps the most perceptive of all) Lytton Strachey, have praised and analysed, there is not much left to say about Sir Thomas Browne's style in general, nor about these two masterpieces in particular, that has not been said better before. I shall therefore stand between the reader and the author no longer than to aver that this text is as accurate as I can make it; to thank my learned friends Sir Geoffrey Keynes, Dr Jeremiah Finch, Mr John Sparrow and the late John Hayward for their advice (none the less warmly where I have not taken it) on half a dozen points of exegesis; and to offer a grateful and affectionate salute, across the years and now all those long miles to Grundisburgh, to the Eton master who first opened a schoolboy's ears to Sir Thomas Browne's music.

CHELSEA
Michaelmas 1957

HYDRIOTAPHIA
URNE BURIALL
OR
A BRIEF DISCOURSE
OF THE SEPULCHRALL URNES
LATELY FOUND IN
NORFOLK

HYDRIOTAPHIA,
URNE-BURIALL,
OR,
A Discourse of the Sepulchrall
Urnes lately found in
NORFOLK.

Together with
The Garden of *CYRUS,*
OR THE
Quincunciall, Lozenge, or
Net-work Plantations of the An-
cients, Artificially, Naturally,
Mystically Considered.
With Sundry Observations.

By *Thomas Browne* D. of Physick.

LONDON,
Printed for *Hen. Brome* at the Signe of the
Gun in *Ivy-lane.* 1658.

TO MY
WORTHY AND HONOURED FRIEND
THOMAS LE GROS
OF *CROSTWICK* ESQUIRE

*When the Funerall pyre was out, and the last valediction over,
men took a lasting adieu of their interred Friends, little expecting
the curiosity of future ages should comment upon their ashes, and
having no old experience of the duration of their Reliques, held
no opinion of such after considerations.*

*But who knows the fate of his bones, or how often he is to be
buried? who hath the Oracle of his ashes, or whither they are to
be scattered? The Reliques of many lie like the ruines of* Pompeys,
*in all parts of the earth; And when they arrive at your hands,
these may seem to have wandred far, who in a direct and*
Meridian *Travell, have but few miles of known Earth between
your self and the Pole.*

That the bones of Theseus *should be seen again in* Athens,
*was not beyond conjecture, and hopeful expectation; but that these
should arise so opportunely to serve your self, was an hit of fate
and honour beyond prediction.*

*We cannot but wish these Urnes might have the effect of
Theatrical vessels, and great* Hippodrome *Urnes in* Rome; *to
resound the acclamations and honour due unto you. But these
are sad and sepulchral Pitchers, which have no joyful voices;
silently expressing old mortality, the ruines of forgotten times,
and can only speak with life, how long in this corruptible frame,
some parts may be uncorrupted; yet able to out-last bones long
unborn, and noblest pyle among us.*

*We present not these as any strange sight or spectacle un-
known to your eyes, who have beheld the best of Urnes, and*

3

noblest variety of Ashes; Who are your self no slender master of Antiquities, and can daily command the view of so many Imperiall faces; Which raiseth your thoughts unto old things, and consideration of times before you, when even living men were Antiquities; when the living might exceed the dead, and to depart this world, could not be properly said, to go unto the greater number. And so run up your thoughts upon the ancient of dayes, the Antiquaries truest object, unto whom the eldest parcels are young, and earth it self an Infant; and without Ægyptian account makes but small noise in thousands.

We were hinted by the occasion, not catched the opportunity to write of old things, or intrude upon the Antiquary. We are coldly drawn unto discourses of Antiquities, who have scarce time before us to comprehend new things, or make out learned Novelties. But seeing they arose as they lay, almost in silence among us, at least in short account suddenly passed over; we were very unwilling they should die again, and be buried twice among us.

Beside, to preserve the living, and make the dead to live, to keep men out of their Urnes, and discourse of humane fragments in them, is not impertinent unto our profession; whose study is life and death, who daily behold examples of mortality, and of all men least need artificial memento's, or coffins by our bed side, to minde us of our graves.

'Tis time to observe Occurrences, and let nothing remarkable escape us; The Supinity of elder dayes hath left so much in silence, or time hath so martyred the Records, that the most industrious heads do finde no easie work to erect a new Britannia.

'Tis opportune to look back upon old times, and contemplate our Forefathers. Great examples grow thin, and to be fetched from the passed world. Simplicity flies away, and iniquity comes at long strides upon us. We have enough to do to make up our selves from present and passed times, and the whole stage of things scarce serveth for our instruction. A compleat peece of

vertue must be made up from the Centos *of all ages, as all the beauties of* Greece *could make but one handsome* Venus.

When the bones of King Arthur *were digged up, the old Race might think, they beheld therein some Originals of themselves; Unto these of our Urnes none here can pretend relation, and can only behold the Reliques of those persons, who in their life giving the Law unto their predecessors, after long obscurity, now lye at their mercies. But remembring the early civility they brought upon these Countreys, and forgetting long passed mischiefs; We mercifully preserve their bones, and pisse not upon their ashes.*

In the offer of these Antiquities we drive not at ancient Families, so long out-lasted by them; We are farre from erecting your worth upon the pillars of your Fore-fathers, whose merits you illustrate. We honour your old Virtues, conformable unto times before you, which are the Noblest Armoury. And having long experience of your friendly conversation, void of empty Formality, full of freedome, constant and Generous Honesty, I look upon you as a Gemme of the Old Rock, and must professe my self even to Urne and Ashes,

Your ever faithfull Friend,

and Servant,

Norwich
May 1

Thomas Browne.

En Sum quod digitis Quinque Levatur onus Propert

URNE BURIALL

CHAPTER I

IN the deep discovery of the Subterranean world, a shallow part would satisfie some enquirers; who, if two or three yards were open about the surface, would not care to rake the bowels of *Potosi*, and regions towards the Centre. Nature hath furnished one part of the Earth, and man another. The treasures of time lie high, in Urnes, Coynes, and Monuments, scarce below the roots of some vegetables. Time hath endlesse rarities, and shows of all varieties; which reveals old things in heaven, makes new discoveries in earth, and even earth it self a discovery. That great Antiquity *America* lay buried for thousands of years; and a large part of the earth is still in the Urne unto us.

Though if *Adam* were made out of an extract of the Earth, all parts might challenge a restitution, yet few have returned their bones farre lower than they might receive them; not affecting the graves of Giants, under hilly and heavy coverings, but content with lesse than their owne depth, have wished their bones might lie soft, and the earth be light upon them; Even such as hope to rise again, would not be content with centrall interrment, or so desperately to place their reliques as to lie beyond discovery, and in no way to be seen again; which happy contrivance hath made communication with our forefathers, and left unto our view some parts, which they never beheld themselves.

Though earth hath engrossed the name yet water hath proved the smartest grave; which in forty dayes swallowed almost mankinde, and the living creation; Fishes not wholly escaping, except the Salt Ocean were handsomely contempered by admixture of the fresh Element.

Many have taken voluminous pains to determine the state of the soul upon disunion; but men have been most phantasticall in the singular contrivances of their corporall dissolution; whilest the sobrest Nations have rested in two wayes, of simple inhumation and burning.

That carnall interment or burying, was of the elder date, the old examples of *Abraham* and the Patriarchs are sufficient to illustrate; And were without competition, if it could be made out, that *Adam* was buried near *Damascus*, or Mount *Calvary*, according to some Tradition. God himself, that buried but one, was pleased to make choice of this way, collectible from Scripture-expression, and the hot contest between Satan and the Arch-Angel, about discovering the body of *Moses*. But the practice of Burning was also of great Antiquity, and of no slender extent. For (not to derive the same from *Hercules*) noble descriptions there are hereof in the Grecian Funerals of *Homer*, In the formall Obsequies of *Patroclus*, and *Achilles*; and somewhat elder in the *Theban* warre, and solemn combustion of *Meneceus*, and *Archemorus*, contemporary unto *Jair* the Eighth Judge of *Israel*. Confirmable also among the *Trojans*, from the Funerall Pyre of *Hector*, burnt before the gates of *Troy*, And the burning of *Penthisilea* the *Amazonean Queen*: and long continuance of that practice, in the inward Countries of *Asia*; while as low as the Reign of *Julian*, we finde that the King of *Chionia* burnt the body of his Son, and interred the ashes in a silver Urne.

The same practice extended also farre West, and besides *Herulians, Getes*, and *Thracians*, was in use with most of the *Celtæ, Sarmatians, Germans, Gauls, Danes, Swedes, Norwegians;* not to omit some use thereof among *Carthaginians*

8

and *Americans*: Of greater Antiquity among the *Romans* than most opinion, or *Pliny* seems to allow. For (beside the old Table Laws of burning or burying within the City, of making the Funerall fire with plained wood, or quenching the fire with wine) *Manlius* the Consul burnt the body of his Son: *Numa* by speciall clause of his Will, was not burnt but buried; And *Remus* was solemnly burned, according to the description of *Ovid*.

Cornelius Sylla was not the first whose body was burned in *Rome*, but of the *Cornelian* Family, which being indifferently, not frequently used before, from that time spread, and became the prevalent practice. Not totally pursued in the highest runne of Cremation; For when even Crows were funerally burnt, *Poppæa* the Wife of *Nero* found a peculiar grave enterment. Now as all customes were founded upon some bottome of Reason, so there wanted not grounds for this; according to severall apprehensions of the most rationall dissolution. Some being of the opinion of *Thales*, that water was the originall of all things, thought it most equall to submit unto the principle of putrefaction, and conclude in a moist relentment. Others conceived it most natural to end in fire, as due unto the master principle in the composition, according to the doctrine of *Heraclitus*. And therefore heaped up large piles, more actively to waft them toward that Element, whereby they also declined a visible degeneration into worms, and left a lasting parcell of their composition.

Some apprehended a purifying virtue in fire, refining the grosser commixture, and firing out the Æthereall particles so deeply immersed in it. And such as by tradition or rationall conjecture held any hint of the finall pyre of all things; or that this Element at last must be too hard for all the rest; might conceive most naturally of the fiery dissolution. Others pretending no natural grounds, politickly declined the malice of enemies upon their buried bodies. Which consideration led *Sylla* unto this practise; who having thus served the body of *Marius*, could not but fear a retaliation upon his own, entertained after in the Civill wars, and revengeful contentions of *Rome*.

But as many Nations embraced, and many left it indifferent, so others too much affected, or strictly declined this practice. The *Indian Brachmans* seemed too great friends unto fire, who burnt themselves alive, and thought it the noblest way to end their dayes in fire; according to the expression of the Indian, burning himself at *Athens*, in his last words upon the pyre unto the amazed spectators, *Thus I make my selfe Immortall.*

But the *Chaldeans*, the great Idolaters of fire, abhorred the burning of their carcasses, as a pollution of that Deity. The *Persian Magi* declined it upon the like scruple, and being only sollicitous about their bones, exposed their flesh to the prey of Birds and Dogges. And the *Persees* now in *India*, which expose their bodies unto Vultures, and endure not so much as *feretra* or Beers of Wood, the proper Fuell of fire, are led on with such niceties. But whether the ancient *Germans* who burned their dead, held any such fear to pollute their Deity of *Herthus*, or the earth, we have no Authentick conjecture.

The Ægyptians were afraid of fire, not as a Deity, but a devouring Element, mercilesly consuming their bodies, and leaving too little of them; and therefore by precious Embalments, depositure in dry earths, or handsome inclosure in glasses, contrived the notablest wayes of integrall conservation. And from such Ægyptian scruples imbibed by *Pythagoras*, it may be conjectured that *Numa* and the Pythagoricall Sect first waved the fiery solution.

The *Scythians* who swore by winde and sword, that is, by life and death, were so farre from burning their bodies, that they declined all interrment, and made their graves in the ayr:

And the *Ichthyophagi* or fish-eating Nations about Ægypt, affected the Sea for their grave: Thereby declining visible corruption, and restoring the debt of their bodies. Whereas the old Heroes in *Homer* dreaded nothing more than water or drowning; probably upon the old opinion of the fiery substance of the soul, only extinguishable by that Element; And therefore the Poet emphatically implieth the totall destruction in this kinde of death, which happened to *Ajax Oileus*.

The old *Balearians* had a peculiar mode, for they used great Urnes and much wood, but no fire in their burials, while they bruised the flesh and bones of the dead, crowded them into Urnes, and laid heapes of wood upon them. And the *Chinois* without cremation or urnall interrment of their bodies, make use of trees and much burning, while they plant a Pine-tree by their grave, and burn great numbers of printed draughts of slaves and horses over it, civilly content with their companies in effigie, which barbarous Nations exact unto reality.

Christians abhorred this way of obsequies, and though they stickt not to give their bodies to be burnt in their lives, detested that mode after death; affecting rather a depositure than absumption, and properly submitting unto the sentence of God, to return not unto ashes but unto dust againe, conformable unto the practice of the Patriarchs, the interrment of our Saviour, of *Peter*, *Paul*, and the ancient Martyrs. And so farre at last declining promiscuous enterrment with Pagans, that some have suffered Ecclesiastical censures, for making no scruple thereof.

The *Musselman* beleevers will never admit this fiery resolution. For they hold a present trial from their black and white Angels in the grave; which they must have made so hollow, that they may rise upon their knees.

The Jewish Nation, though they entertained the old way of inhumation, yet sometimes admitted this practice. For the men of *Jabesh* burnt the body of *Saul*. And by no prohibited practice, to avoid contagion or pollution, in time of pestilence, burnt the bodies of their friends. And when they burnt not their dead bodies, yet sometimes used great burnings neare and about them, deducible from the expressions concerning *Jehoram, Sedechias,* and the sumptuous pyre of *Asa*: And were so little averse from Pagan burning, that the Jews lamenting the death of *Cæsar* their friend, and revenger on *Pompey,* frequented the place where his body was burnt for many nights together. And as they raised noble Monuments and *Mausolæums* for their own Nation, so they were not scrupulous in erecting some for others, according to the practice of *Daniel,* who left that lasting sepulchrall pyle in *Echbatana,* for the *Medean* and *Persian* Kings.

But even in times of subjection and hottest use, they conformed not unto the *Romane* practice of burning; whereby the Prophecy was secured concerning the body of Christ, that it should not see corruption, or a bone should not be broken; which we beleeve was also providentially prevented, from the Souldiers spear and nails that past by the little bones both in his hands and feet: Nor of ordinary contrivance, that it should not corrupt on the Crosse, according to the Laws of *Romane* Crucifixion, or an hair of his head perish, though observable in Jewish customes, to cut the hairs of Malefactors.

Nor in their long co-habitation with Ægyptians, crept into a custome of their exact embalming, wherein deeply slashing the muscles, and taking out the brains and entrails, they had broken the subject of so entire a Resurrection, nor fully answered the types of *Enoch, Eliah,* or *Jonah,* which yet to prevent or restore, was of equall facility unto that rising power, able to break the fasciations and bands of death, to get clear out of the Cere-cloth, and an hundred pounds of oyntment, and out of the Sepulchre before the stone was rolled from it.

But though they embraced not this practice of burning, yet entertained they many ceremonies agreeable unto *Greeke* and *Romane* obsequies. And he that observeth their funerall Feasts, their Lamentations at the grave, their musick, and weeping mourners; how they closed the eyes of their friends, how they washed, anointed, and kissed the dead; may easily conclude these were not meere Pagan-Civilities. But whether that mournfull burthen, and treble calling out after *Absalom*, had any reference unto the last conclamation, and triple valediction, used by other Nations, we hold but a wavering conjecture.

Civilians make sepulture but of the Law of Nations, others doe naturally found it and discover it also in animals. They that are so thick skinned as still to credit the story of the *Phœnix*, may say something for animall burning: More serious conjectures finde some examples of sepulture in Elephants, Cranes, the Sepulchrall Cells of Pismires and practice of Bees; which civill society carrieth out their dead, and hath exequies, if not interrments.

CHAPTER II

THE Solemnities, Ceremonies, Rites of their Cremation or enterrment, so solemnly delivered by Authours, we shall not disparage our Reader to repeat. Only the last and lasting part in their Urns, collected bones and Ashes, we cannot wholly omit, or decline that Subject, which occasion lately presented, in some discovered among us.

In a Field of old *Walsingham*, not many moneths past, were digged up between fourty and fifty Urnes, deposited in a dry and sandy soile, not a yard deep, nor farre from one another: Not all strictly of one figure, but most answering these described: Some containing two pounds of bones, distinguishable in skulls, ribs, jawes, thigh-bones, and teeth, with fresh impressions of their combustion. Besides the extraneous substances, like peeces of small boxes, or combes handsomely wrought, handles of small brasse instruments, brazen nippers, and in one some kinde of *Opale*.

Near the same plot of ground, for about six yards compasse were digged up coals and incinerated substances, which begat conjecture that this was the *Ustrina* or place of burning their bodies, or some sacrificing place unto the *Manes*, which was properly below the surface of the ground, as the *Aræ* and Altars unto the gods and *Heroes* above it.

That these were the Urnes of *Romanes* from the common custome and place where they were found, is no obscure conjecture, not farre from a *Romane* Garrison, and but five Miles from *Brancaster*, set down by ancient Record under the name of *Brannodunum*. And where the adjoyning Towne, containing seven Parishes, in no very different sound, but Saxon Termination, still retains the Name of *Burnham*, which being an early station, it is not improbable the neighbour

14

parts were filled with habitations, either of *Romanes* themselves, or *Brittains Romanised*, which observed the *Romane* customes.

Nor is it improbable that the *Romanes* early possessed this Countrey; for though we meet not with such strict particulars of these parts, before the new Institution of *Constantine*, and military charge of the Count of the *Saxon* shore, and that about the *Saxon* Invasions, the *Dalmatian* Horsemen were in the Garrison of *Brancaster*: Yet in the time of *Claudius*, *Vespasian*, and *Severus*, we finde no lesse than three Legions dispersed through the Province of *Brittain*. And as high as the Reign of *Claudius* a great overthrow was given unto the *Iceni*, by the *Romane* Lieutenant *Ostorius*. Not long after the Countrey was so molested, that in hope of a better state, *Prasutagus* bequeathed his Kingdome unto *Nero* and his Daughters; and *Boadicea* his Queen fought the last decisive Battle with *Paulinus*. After which time and Conquest of *Agricola* the Lieutenant of *Vespasian*, probable it is they wholly possessed this Countrey, ordering it into Garrisons or Habitations, best suitable with their securities. And so some *Romane* Habitations, not improbable in these parts, as high as the time of *Vespasian*, where the *Saxons* after seated, in whose thin-fill'd Mappes we yet finde the Name of *Walsingham*. Now if the *Iceni* were but *Gammadims*, *Anconians*, or men that lived in an Angle wedge or Elbow of *Brittain*, according to the Originall Etymologie, this country will challenge the Emphaticall appellation, as most properly making the Elbow or Iken of *Icenia*.

That *Britain* was notably populous is undeniable, from that expression of *Cæsar*. That the *Romans* themselves were early in no small Numbers, Seventy Thousand with their associats slain by *Boadicea*, affords a sure account. And though many *Roman* habitations are now unknowne, yet some by old works, Rampiers, Coynes, and Urnes doe testifie their Possessions. Some Urnes have been found at *Castor*, some also about *Southcreake*, and not many years past, no lesse than ten in a Field at *Buxton*, not near any recorded Garison. Nor is it strange to finde *Romane* Coynes of Copper and Silver among us; of *Vespasian, Trajan, Adrian, Commodus, Antoninus, Severus*, &c. But the greater number of *Dioclesian, Constantine, Constans, Valens*, with many of *Victorinus, Posthumius, Tetricus*, and the thirty Tyrants in the Reigne of *Gallienus*; and some as high as *Adrianus* have been found about *Thetford*, or *Sitomagus*, mentioned in the itinerary of *Antoninus*, as the way from *Venta* or *Castor* unto *London*. But the most frequent discovery is made at the two *Casters* by *Norwich* and *Yarmouth*, at *Burghcastle* and *Brancaster*.

Besides the *Norman, Saxon* and *Danish* peeces of *Cuthred, Canutus, William, Matilda*, and others, som Brittish Coynes of gold have been dispersedly found; And no small number of silver peeces near *Norwich*; with a rude head upon the obverse, and an ill formed horse on the reverse, with Inscriptions *Ic. Duro. T.* whether implying *Iceni, Durotriges, Tascia*, or *Trinobantes*, we leave to higher conjecture. Vulgar Chronology will have *Norwich* Castle as old as *Julius Cæsar*; but his distance from these parts, and its *Gothick* form of structure, abridgeth such Antiquity. The *British* Coyns afford conjecture of early habitation in these parts, though the City of *Norwich* arose from the ruines of *Venta*, and though perhaps not without some habitation before, was enlarged, builded, and nominated by the *Saxons*. In what bulk or populosity it stood in the old East-angle Monarchy, tradition and history are silent. Considerable it was in the *Danish* Eruptions, when *Sueno* burnt *Thetford* and *Norwich*, and *Ulfketel* the Governour thereof was able to make some resistance, and after endeavoured to burn the *Danish* Navy.

How the *Romanes* left so many Coynes in Countreys of

their Conquests, seems of hard resolution, except we consider how they buried them under ground, when upon barbarous invasions they were fain to desert their habitations in most part of their Empire; and the strictnesse of their laws forbidding to transfer them to any other uses; Wherein the *Spartans* were singular, who to make their Copper money uselesse, contempered it with vinegar. That the *Brittains* left any, some wonder; since their money was iron, and Iron rings before *Cæsar*; and those of after stamp by permission, and but small in bulk and bignesse. That so few of the *Saxons* remain, because overcome by succeeding Conquerours upon the place, their Coynes by degrees passed into other stamps, and the marks of after ages.

Than the time of these Urnes deposited, or precise Antiquity of these Reliques, nothing of more uncertainty. For since the Lieutenant of *Claudius* seems to have made the first progresse into these parts, since *Boadicea* was overthrown by the Forces of *Nero*, and *Agricola* put a full end to these Conquests; it is not probable the Countrey was fully garrison'd or planted before; and therefore however these Urnes might be of later date, not likely of higher Antiquity.

And the succeeding Emperours desisted not from their Conquests in these and other parts; as testified by history and medall inscription yet extant. The Province of *Brittain* in so divided a distance from *Rome*, beholding the faces of many Imperiall persons, and in large account no fewer than *Cæsar, Claudius, Britannicus, Vespasian, Titus, Adrian, Severus, Commodus, Geta*, and *Caracalla*.

A great obscurity herein, because no medall or Emperours Coyne enclosed, which might denote the date of their enterrments; observable in many Urnes, and found in those of *Spittle* Fields by *London*, which contained the Coynes of *Claudius, Vespasian, Commodus, Antoninus*, attended with

17

Lacrymatories, Lamps, Bottles of Liquor, and other appurtenances of affectionate superstition, which in these rurall
interrements were wanting.

Some uncertainty there is from the period or term of
burning, or the cessation of that practise. *Macrobius* affirmeth
it was disused in his dayes. But most agree, though without
authentick record, that it ceased with the *Antonini*. Most
safely to be understood, after the Reigne of those Emperours
which assumed the name of *Antoninus*, extending unto
Heliogabalus. Not strictly after *Marcus*; For about fifty years
later we finde the magnificent burning, and consecration of
Severus; and if we so fix this period or cessation, these Urnes
will challenge above thirteen hundred years.

But whether this practise was onely then left by Emperours
and great persons, or generally about *Rome*, and not in other
Provinces, we hold no authentick account. For after *Ter-
tullian*, in the dayes of *Minucius* it was obviously objected
upon Christians, that they condemned the practise of burning.
And we finde a passage in *Sidonius*, which asserteth that
practise in *France* unto a lower account. And perhaps not
fully disused till Christianity fully established, which gave the
finall extinction to these sepulchrall Bonefires.

Whether they were the bones of men or women or children,
no authentick decision from ancient custome in distinct places
of buriall. Although not improbably conjectured, that the
double Sepulture or burying place of *Abraham*, had in it such
intension. But from exility of bones, thinnesse of skulls, smallnesse of teeth, ribbes, and thigh-bones; not improbable that
many thereof were persons of *minor* age, or women. Confirmable also from things contained in them: In most were
found substances resembling Combes, Plates like Boxes,
fastened with Iron pins, and handsomely overwrought like
the necks or Bridges of Musicall Instruments, long brasse

plates overwrought like the handles of neat implements, brazen nippers to pull away hair, and in one a kinde of *Opale* yet maintaining a blewish colour.

Now that they accustomed to burn or bury with them things wherein they excelled, delighted, or which were dear unto them, either as farewells unto all pleasure, or vain apprehension that they might use them in the other world, is testified by all Antiquity. Observable from the Gemme or Berill Ring upon the finger of *Cynthia*, the Mistresse of *Propertius*, when after her Funerall Pyre her Ghost appeared unto him. And notably illustrated from the Contents of that *Romane* Urne preserved by Cardinall *Farnese*, wherein besides great number of Gemmes with heads of Gods and Goddesses, were found an Ape of *Agath*, a Grashopper, an Elephant of Ambre, a Crystall Ball, three glasses, two Spoones, and six Nuts of Crystall. And beyond the content of Urnes, in the Monument of *Childerick* the first, and fourth King from *Pharamond*, casually discovered three years past at *Tournay*, restoring unto the world much gold richly adorning his Sword, two hundred Rubies, many hundred Imperial Coyns, three hundred golden Bees, the bones and horseshoe of his horse enterred with him, according to the barbarous magnificence of those dayes in their sepulchral Obsequies. Although if we steer by the conjecture of many and Septuagint expression; some trace thereof may be found even with the ancient Hebrews, not only from the Sepulcrall treasure of *David*, but the circumcision knives which *Josuah* also buried.

Some men considering the contents of these Urnes, lasting peeces and toyes included in them, and the custome of burning with many other Nations, might somewhat doubt whether all Urnes found among us were properly *Romane* Reliques, or some not belonging unto our *Brittish*, *Saxon*, or *Danish* Forefathers.

In the form of Buriall among the ancient *Brittains*, the large Discourses of *Cæsar*, *Tacitus*, and *Strabo* are silent: For the discovery whereof, with other particulars, we much deplore the losse of that Letter which *Cicero* expected or received from his Brother *Quintus*, as a resolution of *Brittish* customes; or the account which might have been made by *Scribonius Largus*, the Physician accompanying the Emperour *Claudius*, who might have also discovered that frugall Bit of the Old *Brittains*, which in the bignesse of a Bean could satisfie their thirst and hunger.

But that the *Druids* and ruling Priests used to burn and bury, is expressed by *Pomponius*; That *Bellinus* the Brother of *Brennus* and King of *Brittains* was burnt, is acknowledged by *Polydorus*. That they held that practise in *Gallia*, *Cæsar* expresly delivereth. Whether the *Brittains* (probably descended from them, of like Religion, Language and Manners) did not sometimes make use of burning; or whether at least such as were after civilized unto the *Romane* life and manners, conformed not unto this practise, we have not historicall assertion or deniall. But since from the account of *Tacitus* the *Romanes* early wrought so much civility upon the British stock, that they brought them to build Temples, to wear the Gowne, and study the *Romane* Laws and language, that they conformed also unto their religious rites and customes in burials, seems no improbable conjecture.

That burning the dead was used in *Sarmatia*, is affirmed by *Gaguinus*, that the *Sueons* and *Gothlanders* used to burne their Princes and great persons, is delivered by *Saxo* and *Olaus*; that this was the old *Germane* practise, is also asserted by *Tacitus*. And though we are bare in historicall particulars of such obsequies in this Island, or that the *Saxons*, *Jutes*, and *Angles* burnt their dead, yet came they from parts where 'twas of ancient practise; the *Germanes* using it, from whom they were descended. And even in *Jutland* and *Sleswick* in *Anglia Cymbrica*, Urnes with bones were found not many years before us.

But the *Danish* and Northern Nations have raised an *Æra* or point of compute from their Custome of burning their dead: Some deriving it from *Unguinus*, some from *Frotho* the great; who ordained by Law, that Princes and Chief Commanders should be committed unto the fire, though the common sort had the common grave enterrment. So *Starkatterus* that old *Heroe* was burnt, and *Ringo* royally burnt the body of *Harald* the King slain by him.

What time this custome generally expired in that Nation, we discern no assured period; whether it ceased before Christianity, or upon their Conversion, by *Ansgarius* the Gaul in the time of *Ludovicus Pius* the Sonne of *Charles* the great, according to good computes; or whether it might not be used by some persons, while for a hundred and eighty years Paganisme and Christianity were promiscuously embraced among them, there is no assured conclusion. About which times the *Danes* were busie in *England*, and particularly infested this Countrey: Where many Castles and strong holds were built by them, or against them, and great number of names and Families still derived from them. But since this custome was probably disused before their Invasion or Conquest, and the *Romanes* confessedly practised the same, since their possession of this Island, the most assured account will fall upon the *Romanes*, or *Brittains Romanized*.

However, certain it is, that Urnes conceived of no *Romane* Originall, are often digged up both in *Norway*, and *Denmark*, handsomely described, and graphically represented by the Learned Physician *Wormius*, And in some parts of *Denmark* in no ordinary number, as stands delivered by Authours exactly describing those Countreys. And they contained not only bones, but many other substances in them, as Knives, peeces of Iron, Brasse and Wood, and one of *Norwaye* a brasse guilded Jewes-harp.

Nor were they confused or carelesse in disposing the noblest sort, while they placed large stones in circle about the Urnes, or bodies which they interred: Somewhat answerable unto the Monument of *Rollrich* stones in *England*, or sepulcrall Monument probably erected by *Rollo*, who after conquered *Normandy*. Where 'tis not improbable somewhat might be discovered. Mean while to what Nation or person belonged that large Urne found at *Ashburie*, containing mighty bones, and a Buckler; What those large Urnes found at little *Massing-ham*, or why the *Anglesea* Urnes are placed with their mouths downward, remains yet undiscovered.

CHAPTER III

PLAYSTERED and whited Sepulchres were anciently affected in cadaverous and corruptive Burials; And the rigid Jews were wont to garnish the Sepulchres of the righteous; *Ulysses* in *Hecuba* cared not how meanly he lived, so he might finde a noble Tomb after death. Great Persons affected great Monuments, And the fair and larger Urnes contained no vulgar ashes, which makes that disparity in those which time discovereth among us. The present Urnes were not of one capacity, the largest containing above a gallon, Some not much above half that measure; nor all of one figure, wherein there is no strict conformity, in the same or different Countreys; Observable from those represented by *Casalius*, *Bosio*, and others, though all found in *Italy*: While many have handles, ears, and long necks, but most imitate a circular figure, in a sphericall and round composure; whether from any mystery, best duration or capacity, were but a conjecture. But the common form with necks was a proper figure, making our last bed like our first; nor much unlike the Urnes of our Nativity, while we lay in the nether part of the Earth, and inward vault of our Microcosme. Many Urnes are red, these but of a black colour, somewhat smooth, and dully sounding, which begat some doubt, whether they were burnt, or only baked in Oven or Sunne: According to the ancient way, in many bricks, tiles, pots, and testaceous works; and as the word *testa* is properly to be taken, when occurring without addition: And chiefly intended by *Pliny*, when he commendeth bricks and tiles of two years old, and to make them in the spring. Nor only these concealed peeces, but the open magnificence of Antiquity, ran much in the Artifice of Clay. Hereof the house of *Mausolus* was built, thus old *Jupiter* stood in the Capitoll, and the

Statua of *Hercules* made in the Reign of *Tarquinius Priscus*, was extant in *Plinies* dayes. And such as declined burning or Funerall Urnes, affected Coffins of Clay, according to the mode of *Pythagoras*, and way preferred by *Varro*. But the spirit of great ones was above these circumscriptions, affecting copper, silver, gold, and *Porphyrie* Urnes, wherein *Severus* lay, after a serious view and sentence on that which should contain him. Some of these Urnes were thought to have been silvered over, from sparklings in several pots, with small Tinsell parcels; uncertain whether from the earth, or the first mixture in them.

Among these Urnes we could obtain no good account of their coverings; Only one seemed arched over with some kinde of brickwork. Of those found at *Buxton* some were covered with flints, some in other parts with tiles, those at *Yarmouth Caster* were closed with *Romane* bricks. And some have proper earthen covers adapted and fitted to them. But in the *Homericall* Urne of *Patroclus*, whatever was the solid Tegument, we finde the immediate covering to be a purple peece of silk: And such as had no covers might have the earth closely pressed into them, after which disposure were probably some of these, wherein we found the bones and ashes half mortered unto the sand and sides of the Urne; and some long roots of Quich, or Dogs-grass wreathed about the bones.

No Lamps, included Liquors, Lachrymatories, or Tear-bottles attended these rurall Urnes, either as sacred unto the *Manes*, or passionate expressions of their surviving friends. While with rich flames and hired tears they solemnized their Obsequies, and in the most lamented Monuments made one part of their Inscriptions. Some finde sepulchrall Vessels containing liquors, which time hath incrassated into gellies. For beside these Lachrymatories, notable Lamps with Vessels

of Oyles and Aromaticall Liquors attended noble Ossuaries
And some yet retaining a Vinosity and spirit in them, which
if any have tasted they have farre exceeded the Palats of
Antiquity. Liquors not to be computed by years of annuall
Magistrates, but by great conjunctions and the fatall periods
of Kingdomes. The draughts of Consulary date were but
crude unto these, and *Opimian* Wine but in the must unto
them.

In sundry Graves and Sepulchres, we meet with Rings,
Coynes, and Chalices; Ancient frugality was so severe, that
they allowed no gold to attend the Corps, but only that which
served to fasten their teeth. Whether the *Opaline* stone in
this Urne were burnt upon the finger of the dead, or cast into
the fire by some affectionate friend, it will consist with either
custome. But other incinerable substances were found so
fresh, that they could feel no sindge from fire. These upon
view were judged to be wood, but sinking in water and tried
by the fire, we found them to be bone or Ivory. In their
hardnesse and yellow colour they most resembled Box, which
in old expressions found the Epithete of Eternall, and perhaps in such conservatories might have passed uncorrupted.

That Bay-leaves were found green in the Tomb of S. *Hum-
bert*, after an hundred and fifty years, was looked upon as
miraculous. Remarkable it was unto old Spectators, that the
Cypresse of the Temple of *Diana* lasted so many hundred
years: The wood of the Ark and Olive Rod of *Aaron* were
older at the Captivity. But the Cypresse of the Ark of *Noah*
was the greatest vegetable Antiquity, if *Josephus* were not
deceived by some fragments of it in his dayes. To omit the
Moore-logs, and Firretrees found under-ground in many
parts of *England*; the undated ruines of windes, flouds or
earthquakes; and which in *Flanders* still shew from what
quarter they fell, as generally lying in a North-East position.

But though we found not these peeces to be Wood, according to first apprehension, yet we missed not altogether of some woody substance; For the bones were not·so clearly pickt, but some coals were found amongst them; A way to make wood perpetuall, and a fit associat for metall, whereon was laid the foundation of the great *Ephesian* Temple, and which were made the lasting tests of old boundaries and Landmarks; Whilest we look on these, we admire not Observations of Coals found fresh, after four hundred years. In a long deserted habitation, even Egge-shels have been found fresh, not tending to corruption.

In the Monument of King *Childerick*, the Iron Reliques were found all rusty and crumbling into peeces. But our little Iron pins which fastened the Ivory works, held well together, and lost not their Magneticall quality, though wanting a tenacious moisture for the firmer union of parts; although it be hardly drawn into fusion, yet that metall soon submitteth unto rust and dissolution. In the brazen peeces we admired not the duration but the freedome from rust and ill savour, upon the hardest attrition; but now exposed unto the piercing Atomes of ayre, in the space of a few moneths, they begin to spot and betray their green entrals. We conceive not these Urnes to have descended thus naked as they appear, or to have entred their graves without the old habit of flowers. The Urne of *Philopœmen* was so laden with flowers and ribbons, that it afforded no sight of it self. The rigid *Lycurgus* allowed Olive and Myrtle. The *Athenians* might fairly except against the practise of *Democritus* to be buried up in honey; as fearing to embezzle a great commodity of their Countrey, and the best of that kinde in *Europe*. But *Plato* seemed too frugally politick, who allowed no larger Monument than would contain four Heroick Verses, and designed the most barren ground for sepulture: Though we cannot commend the goodnesse of that sepulchrall ground, which was set at no higher rate than the mean salary of *Judas*. Though the earth had confounded the ashes of these Ossuaries, yet the bones were so smartly burnt, that some thin plates of brasse were found half melted among them; whereby we apprehend they were not of the meanest carcasses, perfunctorily fired as sometimes in military, and commonly in pestilence, burnings; or after the manner of abject corps, hudled forth and carelesly burnt, without the Esquiline Port at *Rome*; which was an affront contrived upon *Tiberius*, while they but half burnt his body, and in the Amphitheatre, according to the custome in notable Malefactors; whereas *Nero* seemed not so much to feare his death, as that his head should be cut off, and his body not burnt entire.

Some finding many fragments of sculs in these Urnes, suspected a mixture of bones; In none we searched was there cause of such conjecture, though sometimes they declined not that practise; The ashes of *Domitian* were mingled with those of *Julia*, of *Achilles* with those of *Patroclus*: All Urnes contained not single Ashes; Without confused burnings they affectionately compounded their bones; passionately endeavouring to continue their living Unions. And when distance of death denied such conjunctions, unsatisfied affections conceived some satisfaction to be neighbours in the grave, to lye Urne by Urne, and touch but in their names. And many were so curious to continue their living relations, that they contrived large, and family Urnes, wherein the Ashes of their nearest friends and kindred might successively be received, at least some parcels thereof, while their collaterall memorials lay in *minor* vessels about them.

Antiquity held too light thoughts from Objects of mortality, while some drew provocatives of mirth from Anatomies, and Juglers shewed tricks with Skeletons. When Fidlers made not so pleasant mirth as Fencers, and men could sit with quiet stomacks while hanging was plaied before them. Old considerations made few *memento's* by sculs and bones upon their monuments. In the Ægyptian Obelisks and Hieroglyphicall figures it is not easie to meet with bones. The sepulchrall Lamps speak nothing lesse than sepulture; and in their literall draughts prove often obscene and antick peeces: Where we finde *D.M.* it is obvious to meet with sacrificing *patera's*, and vessels of libation, upon old sepulchrall Monuments. In the Jewish *Hypogæum* and subterranean Cell at *Rome*, was little observable beside the variety of Lamps, and frequent draughts of the holy Candlestick. In authentick draughts of *Anthony* and *Jerome*, we meet with thigh-bones and deaths heads; but the cemiteriall Cels of ancient Christians and Martyrs, were filled with draughts of Scripture Stories; not declining the flourishes of Cypresse, Palmes, and Olive; and the mysticall Figures of Peacocks, Doves and Cocks. But iterately affecting the pourtraits of *Enoch*, *Laʒarus*, *Jonas*, and the Vision of *Eʒechiel*, as hopefull draughts, and hinting imagery of the Resurrection; which is the life of the grave, and sweetens our habitations in the Land of Moles and Pismires.

Gentile Inscriptions precisely delivered the extent of mens lives, seldome the manner of their deaths, which history it self so often leaves obscure in the records of memorable persons. There is scarce any Philosopher but dies twice or thrice in *Laertius*; Nor almost any life without two or three deaths in *Plutarch*; which makes the tragicall ends of noble persons more favourably resented by compassionate Readers, who finde some relief in the Election of such differences.

The certainty of death is attended with uncertainties, in time, manner, places. The variety of Monuments hath often obscured true graves: and *Cenotaphs* confounded Sepulchres.

For beside their reall Tombs, many have founded honorary and empty Sepulchres. The variety of *Homers* Monuments made him of various Countreys. *Euripides* had his Tomb in *Attica*, but his sepulture in *Macedonia*. And *Severus* found his real Sepulchre in *Rome*, but his empty grave in *Gallia*.

He that lay in a golden Urne eminently above the Earth, was not likely to finde the quiet of these bones. Many of these Urnes were broke by a vulgar discoverer in hope of inclosed treasure. The ashes of *Marcellus* were lost above ground, upon the like account. Where profit hath prompted, no age hath wanted such miners. For which the most barbarous Expilators found the most civill Rhetorick. Gold once out of the earth is no more due unto it; What was unreasonably committed to the ground is reasonably resumed from it: Let Monuments and rich Fabricks, not Riches adorn mens ashes. The commerce of the living is not to be transferred unto the dead: It is no injustice to take that which none complains to lose, and no man is wronged where no man is possessor.

What virtue yet sleeps in this *terra damnata* and aged cinders, were petty magick to experiment; These crumbling reliques and long-fired particles superannuate such expectations: Bones, hairs, nails, and teeth of the dead, were the treasures of old Sorcerers. In vain we revive such practices; Present superstition too visibly perpetuates the folly of our Fore-fathers, wherein unto old Observation this Island was so compleat, that it might have instructed *Persia*.

Plato's historian of the other world lies twelve dayes incorrupted, while his soul was viewing the large stations of the dead. How to keep the corps seven dayes from corruption by anointing and washing, without exenteration, were an hazardable peece of art, in our choisest practise. How they made distinct separation of bones and ashes from fiery admixture, hath found no historicall solution. Though they seemed to make a distinct collection, and overlooked not *Pyrrhus* his toe. Some provision they might make by fictile Vessels, Coverings, Tiles, or flat stones, upon and about the body. And in the same Field, not farre from these Urnes, many stones were found under ground, as also by carefull separation of extraneous matter, composing and raking up the burnt bones with forks, observable in that notable Lamp of *Galvanus*. *Marlianus*, who had the sight of the *Vas Ustrinum*, or vessell wherein they burnt the dead, found in the Esquiline Field at *Rome*, might have afforded clearer solution. But their insatisfaction herein begat that remarkable invention in the Funerall Pyres of some Princes, by incombustible sheets made with a texture of *Asbestos*, incremable flax, or Salamanders wool, which preserved their bones and ashes incommixed.

How the bulk of a man should sink into so few pounds of bones and ashes, may seem strange unto any who considers not its constitution, and how slender a masse will remain upon an open and urging fire of the carnall composition. Even bones themselves reduced into ashes, do abate a notable proportion. And consisting much of a volatile salt, when that is fired out, make a light kind of cinders. Although their bulk be disproportionable to their weight, when the heavy principle of Salt is fired out, and the Earth almost only remaineth; Observable in sallow, which makes more Ashes than Oake; and discovers the common fraud of selling Ashes by measure, and not by ponderation.

Some bones make best Skeletons, some bodies quick and speediest ashes: Who would expect a quick flame from Hydropicall *Heraclitus?* The poysoned Souldier when his Belly brake, put out two pyres in *Plutarch*. But in the plague of *Athens*, one private pyre served two or three Intruders; and the *Saracens* burnt in large heaps, by the King of *Castile*, shewed how little Fuell sufficeth. Though the Funerall pyre of *Patroclus* took up an hundred foot, a peece of an old boat burnt *Pompey*; And if the burthen of *Isaac* were sufficient for an holocaust, a man may carry his owne pyre.

From animals are drawn good burning lights, and good medicines against burning; Though the seminall humour seems of a contrary nature to fire, yet the body compleated proves a combustible lump, wherein fire findes flame even from bones, and some fuell almost from all parts. Though the Metropolis of humidity seems least disposed unto it, which might render the sculls of these Urnes lesse burned than other bones. But all flies or sinks before fire almost in all bodies: When the common ligament is dissolved, the attenuable parts ascend, the rest subside in coal, calx or ashes.

To burn the bones of the King of *Edom* for Lyme, seems no irrationall ferity; But to drink of the ashes of dead relations, a passionate prodigality. He that hath the ashes of his friend, hath an everlasting treasure: where fire taketh leave, corruption slowly enters; In bones well burnt, fire makes a wall against it self; experimented in copels, and tests of metals, which consist of such ingredients. What the Sun compoundeth, fire analyseth, not transmuteth. That devouring agent leaves almost allwayes a morsell for the Earth, whereof all things are but a colonie; and which, if time permits, the mother Element will have in their primitive masse again.

He that looks for Urnes and old sepulchrall reliques, must not seek them in the ruines of Temples; where no Religion anciently placed them. These were found in a Field, according to ancient custome, in noble or private buriall; the old practise of the *Canaanites*, the Family of *Abraham*, and the burying place of *Josua*, in the borders of his possessions; and also agreeable unto *Roman* practice to bury by high-wayes, whereby their Monuments were under eye: Memorials of themselves, and *memento's* of mortality unto living passengers; whom the Epitaphs of great ones were fain to beg to stay and look upon them. A language though sometimes used, not so proper in Church-Inscriptions. The sensible Rhetorick of the dead, to exemplarity of good life, first admitted the bones of pious men and Martyrs within Church-wals; which in succeeding ages crept into promiscuous practise. While *Constantine* was peculiarly favoured to be admitted unto the Church Porch; and the first thus buried in *England* was in the dayes of *Cuthred.*

Christians dispute how their bodies should lye in the grave. In urnall enterrment they clearly escaped this Controversie: Though we decline the Religious consideration, yet in cemiteriall and narrower burying places, to avoid confusion and crosse position, a certain posture were to be admitted; Which even Pagan civility observed. The *Persians* lay North and South, The *Megarians* and *Phœnicians* placed their heads to the East: The *Athenians*, some think, towards the West, which Christians still retain. And *Beda* will have it to be the posture of our Saviour. That he was crucified with his face towards the West, we will not contend with tradition and probable account; but we applaud not the hand of the Painter, in exalting his Crosse so high above those on either side; since hereof we finde no authentick account in history, and even the crosses found by *Helena* pretend no such distinction from longitude or dimension.

To be gnaw'd out of our graves, to have our sculs made drinking-bowls, and our bones turned into Pipes, to delight and sport our Enemies, are Tragicall abominations, escaped in burning Burials.

Urnall enterrments, and burnt Reliques lye not in fear of worms, or to be an heritage for Serpents; In carnall sepulture, corruptions seem peculiar unto parts, and some speak of snakes out of the spinall marrow. But while we suppose common wormes in graves, 'tis not easie to finde any there; few in Church-yards above a foot deep, fewer or none in Churches, though in fresh decayed bodies. Teeth, bones, and hair, give the most lasting defiance to corruption. In an Hydropicall body ten years buried in a Church-yard, we met with a fat concretion, where the nitre of the Earth, and the salt and lixivious liquor of the body, had coagulated large lumps of fat, into the consistence of the hardest castle-soap; whereof part remaineth with us. After a battle with the *Persians* the *Roman* Corps decayed in few dayes, while the *Persian* bodies remained dry and uncorrupted. Bodies in the same ground do not uniformly dissolve, nor bones equally moulder; whereof in the opprobrious disease we expect no long duration. The body of Marquesse of *Dorset* seemed sound and handsomely cereclothed, that after seventy eight years was found uncorrupted. Common Tombs preserve not beyond powder: A firmer consistence and compage of parts might be expected from Arefaction, deep buriall or charcoal. The greatest Antiquities of mortall bodies may remain in petrified bones, whereof, though we take not in the pillar of *Lots* wife, or Metamorphosis of *Ortelius*, some may be older than Pyramids, in the petrified Reliques of the generall inundation. When *Alexander* opened the Tomb of *Cyrus*, the remaining bones discovered his proportion, whereof urnall fragments afford but a bad conjecture, and have this disadvantage of grave enterrments, that they leave us ignorant of most personall discoveries. For since bones afford not only rectitude and stability, but figure unto the body; It is no impossible Physiognomy to conjecture at fleshy appendencies; and after what shape the muscles and carnous parts might hang in their full consistences. A full spread *Cariola* shews a well-shaped

33

horse behinde, handsome formed sculls give some analogie of fleshy resemblance. A criticall view of bones makes a good distinction of sexes. Even colour is not beyond conjecture; since it is hard to be deceived in the distinction of *Negro's* sculls. *Dantes* Characters are to be found in sculls as well as faces. *Hercules* is not onely known by his foot. Other parts make out their comproportions, and inferences upon whole or parts. And since the dimensions of the head measure the whole body, and the figure thereof gives conjecture of the principall faculties; Physiognomy outlives our selves, and ends not in our graves.

Severe contemplators observing these lasting reliques, may think them good monuments of persons past, little advantage to future beings. And considering that power which subdueth all things unto it self, that can resume the scattered Atomes, or identifie out of any thing, conceive it superfluous to expect a resurrection out of Reliques. But the soul subsisting, other matter clothed with due accidents may salve the individuality: Yet the Saints we observe arose from graves and monuments, about the holy City. Some think the ancient Patriarchs so earnestly desired to lay their bones in *Canaan*, as hoping to make a part of that Resurrection, and though thirty miles from Mount *Calvary*, at least to lie in that Region, which should produce the first-fruits of the dead. And if according to learned conjecture, the bodies of men shall rise where their greatest Reliques remain, many are not like to erre in the Topography of their Resurrection, though their bones or bodies be after translated by Angels into the field of *Ezechiels* vision, or as some will order it, into the Valley of Judgement, or *Jehosaphat*.

CHAPTER IV

CHRISTIANS have handsomely glossed the deformity of death, by careful consideration of the body, and civil rites which take off brutall terminations. And though they conceived all reparable by a resurrection, cast not off all care of enterrment. For since the ashes of Sacrifices burnt upon the Altar of God, were carefully carried out by the Priests, and deposed in a clean field; since they acknowledged their bodies to be the lodging of Christ, and temples of the holy Ghost, they devolved not all upon the sufficiency of soul existence; and therefore with long services and full solemnities concluded their last Exequies, wherein to all distinctions the Greek devotion seems most pathetically ceremonious.

Christian invention hath chiefly driven at Rites, which speak hopes of another life, and hints of a Resurrection. And if the ancient Gentiles held not the immortality of their better part, and some subsistence after death; in severall rites, customes, actions and expressions, they contradicted their own opinions: wherein *Democritus* went high, even to the thought of a resurrection, as scoffingly recorded by *Pliny*. What can be more expresse than the expression of *Phocyllides*? Or who would expect from *Lucretius* a sentence of *Ecclisiastes*? Before *Plato* could speak, the soul had wings in *Homer*, which fell not, but flew out of the body into the mansions of the dead; who also observed that handsome distinction of *Demas* and *Soma*, for the body conjoyned to the soul and body separated from it. *Lucian* spoke much truth in jest, when he said, that part of *Hercules* which proceeded from *Alchmena* perished, that from *Jupiter* remained immortall. Thus *Socrates* was content that his friends should bury his body, so they would not think they buried *Socrates*, and regarding only his im-

35

mortall part, was indifferent to be burnt or buried. From such Considerations *Diogenes* might contemn Sepulture. And being satisfied that the soul could not perish, grow carelesse of corporall enterrment. The *Stoicks* who thought the souls of wise men had their habitation about the *moon*, might make slight acccount of subterraneous deposition; whereas the *Pythagorians* and transcorporating Philosophers, who were to be often buried, held great care of their enterrment. And the Platonicks rejected not a due care of the grave, though they put their ashes to unreasonable expectations, in their tedious term of return and long set revolution.

Men have lost their reason in nothing so much as their religion, wherein stones and clouts make Martyrs; and since the religion of one seems madnesse unto another, to afford an account or rationall of old Rites, requires no rigid Reader; That they kindled the pyre aversly, or turning their face from it, was an handsome Symbole of unwilling ministration; That they washed their bones with wine and milk, that the mother wrapt them in Linnen, and dryed them in her bosome, the first fostering part, and place of their nourishment; That they opened their eyes towards heaven, before they kindled the fire, as the place of their hopes or originall, were no improper Ceremonies. Their last valediction thrice uttered by the attendants was also very solemn, and somewhat answered by Christians, who thought it too little, if they threw not the earth thrice upon the enterred body. That in strewing their Tombs the *Romans* affected the Rose, the Greeks *Amaranthus* and myrtle; that the Funerall pyre consisted of sweet fuell, Cypresse, Firre, Larix, Yewe, and Trees perpetually verdant, lay silent expressions of their surviving hopes: Wherein Christians which deck their Coffins with Bays have found a more elegant Embleme. For that tree seeming dead, will restore it self from the root, and its dry and exuccous leaves resume their verdure again; which if we mistake not, we have also observed in furze. Whether the planting of yewe in Churchyards hold not its originall from ancient Funerall rites, or as an Embleme of Resurrection from its perpetual verdure, may also admit conjecture.

They made use of Musick to excite or quiet the affections of their friends, according to different harmonies. But the secret and symbolicall hint was the harmonical nature of the soul; which delivered from the body, went again to enjoy the primitive harmony of heaven, from whence it first descended; which according to its progresse traced by antiquity, came down by *Cancer*, and ascended by *Capricornus*.

They burnt not children before their teeth appeared, as apprehending their bodies too tender a morsell for fire, and that their gristly bones would scarce leave separable reliques after the pyrall combustion. That they kindled not fire in their houses for some dayes after, was a strict memoriall of the late afflicting fire. And mourning without hope, they had an happy fraud against excessive lamentation, by a common opinion that deep sorrows disturbed their ghosts.

That they buried their dead on their backs, or in a supine position, seems agreeable unto profound sleep, and common posture of dying; contrary to the most naturall way of birth; nor like our pendulous posture, in the doubtfull state of the womb. *Diogenes* was singular, who preferred a prone situation in the grave, and some Christians like neither, who decline the figure of rest, and make choice of an erect posture.

That they carried them out of the world with their feet forward, not inconsonant unto reason: As contrary unto the native posture of man, and his production first into it. And also agreeable unto their opinions, while they bid adieu unto the world, not to look again upon it; whereas *Mahometans* who think to return to a delightfull life again, are carried forth with their heads forward, and looking toward their houses.

They closed their eyes as parts which first die or first discover the sad effects of death. But their iterated clamations to excitate their dying or dead friends, or revoke them unto life again, was a vanity of affection; as not presumably ignorant of the criticall tests of death, by apposition of feathers, glasses, and reflexion of figures, which dead eyes represent not; which however not strictly verifiable in fresh and warm *cadavers*, could hardly elude the test, in corps of four or five dayes.

That they suck'd in the last breath of their expiring friends, was surely a practice of no medicall institution, but a loose opinion that the soul passed out that way, and a fondnesse of affection from some *Pythagoricall* foundation, that the spirit of one body passed into another; which they wished might be their own.

That they powred oyle upon the pyre, was a tolerable practise, while the intention rested in facilitating the accension; But to place good *Omens* in the quick and speedy burning, to sacrifice unto the windes for a dispatch in this office, was a low form of superstition.

The *Archimime* or *Jester* attending the Funerall train, and imitating the speeches, gesture, and manners of the deceased, was too light for such solemnities, contradicting their Funerall Orations, and dolefull rites of the grave.

That they buried a peece of money with them as a Fee of the *Elysian Ferriman*, was a practise full of folly. But the ancient custome of placing coynes in considerable Urnes, and the present practise of burying medals in the Noble Foundations of *Europe*, are laudable wayes of historicall discoveries, in actions, persons, Chronologies; and posterity will applaud them.

We examine not the old Laws of Sepulture, exempting certain persons from buriall or burning. But hereby we apprehend that these were not the bones of persons Planet-struck or burnt with fire from Heaven: No Reliques of Traitors to their Countrey, Self-killers, or Sacrilegious Male-factors; Persons in old apprehension unworthy of the *earth*; condemned unto the *Tartarus* of Hell, and bottomlesse pit of *Pluto*, from whence there was no redemption.

Nor were only many customes questionable in order to their Obsequies, but also sundry practises, fictions, and con-ceptions, discordant or obscure, of their state and future beings; whether unto eight or ten bodies of men to adde one of a woman, as being more inflammable, and unctuously constituted for the better pyrall combustion, were any rationall practise: Or whether the complaint of *Perianders* Wife be tolerable, that wanting her Funerall burning she suffered intolerable cold in Hell, according to the constitution of the infernall house of *Pluto*, wherein cold makes a great part of their tortures; it cannot passe without some question.

Why the Female Ghosts appear unto *Ulysses*, before the *Heroes* and masculine spirits? Why the *Psyche* or soul of *Tiresias* is of the masculine gender; who being blinde on earth sees more than all the rest in hell; Why the Funerall Suppers consisted of Egges, Beans, Smallage, and Lettuce, since the dead are made to eat *Asphodels* about the *Elyʒian* medows? Why since there is no Sacrifice acceptable, nor any propitiation for the Covenant of the grave; men set up the Deity of *Morta*, and fruitlesly adored Divinities without ears? it cannot escape some doubt.

The dead seem all alive in the human *Hades* of *Homer*, yet cannot well speak, prophesie, or know the living, except they drink bloud, wherein is the life of man. And therefore the souls of *Penelope's* Paramours conducted by *Mercury* chirped like bats, and those which followed *Hercules* made a noise but like a flock of birds.

The departed spirits know things past and to come, yet are ignorant of things present. *Agamemnon* foretels what should happen unto *Ulysses*, yet ignorantly enquires what is become of his own Son. The Ghosts are afraid of swords in *Homer*, yet *Sybilla* tels *Æneas* in *Virgil*, the thin habit of spirits was beyond the force of weapons. The spirits put off their malice with their bodies, and *Cæsar* and *Pompey* accord in Latine Hell, yet *Ajax* in *Homer* endures not a conference with *Ulysses*: And *Deiphobus* appears all mangled in *Virgils* Ghosts, yet we meet with perfect shadows among the wounded ghosts of *Homer*.

Since *Charon* in *Lucian* applauds his condition among the dead, whether it be handsomely said of *Achilles*, that living contemner of death, that he had rather be a Plowmans servant than Emperour of the dead? How *Hercules* his soul is in hell, and yet in heaven, and *Julius* his soul in a Starre, yet seen by *Æneas* in hell, except the Ghosts were but Images and shadows of the soul, received in higher mansions, according to the ancient division of body, soul, and image or *simulachrum* of them both. The particulars of future beings must needs be dark unto ancient Theories, which Christian Philosophy yet determines but in a Cloud of opinions. A Dialogue between two Infants in the womb concerning the state of this world, might handsomely illustrate our ignorance of the next, whereof methinks we yet discourse in *Platoes* denne, and are but *Embryon* Philosophers.

Pythagoras escapes in the fabulous hell of *Dante*, among that swarm of Philosophers, wherein whilest we meet with *Plato* and *Socrates*, *Cato* is to be found in no lower place than Purgatory. Among all the set, *Epicurus* is most considerable, whom men make honest without an *Elyẓium*, who contemned life without encouragement of immortality, and making nothing after death, yet made nothing of the King of terrours.

Were the happinesse of the next world as closely apprehended as the felicities of this, it were a martyrdome to live;
and unto such as consider none hereafter, it must be more
than death to dye, which makes us amazed at those audacities,
that durst be nothing, and return into their *Chaos* again.
Certainly such spirits as could contemn death, when they
expected no better being after, would have scorned to live
had they known any. And therefore we applaud not the
judgment of *Machiavel*, that Christianity makes men cowards,
or that with the confidence of but half dying, the despised
virtues of patience and humility have abased the spirits of
men, which Pagan principles exalted, but rather regulated
the wildenesse of audacities, in the attempts, grounds, and
eternall sequels of death; wherein men of the boldest spirits
are often prodigiously temerarious. Nor can we extenuate
the valour of ancient Martyrs, who contemned death in the
uncomfortable scene of their lives, and in their decrepit
Martyrdomes did probably lose not many moneths of their
dayes, or parted with life when it was scarce worth the living.
For (beside that long time past holds no consideration unto a
slender time to come) they had no small disadvantage from the
constitution of old age, which naturally makes men fearfull;
complexionally superannuated from the bold and couragious
thoughts of youth and fervent years. But the contempt of death
from corporall animosity promoteth not our felicity. They may
sit in the *Orchestra*, and noblest Seats of Heaven, who have held
up shaking hands in the fire, and humanly contended for glory.

Mean while *Epicurus* lyes deep in *Dante's* hell, wherein we
meet with Tombs enclosing souls which denied their im-
mortalities. But whether the virtuous heathen, who lived
better than he spake, or erring in the principles of himself,
yet lived above Philosophers of more specious Maximes, lye so
deep as he is placed; at least so low as not to rise against

Christians, who beleeving or knowing that truth, have lastingly denied it in their practise and conversation, were a quæry too sad to insist on.

But all or most apprehensions rested in Opinions of some future being, which ignorantly or coldly beleeved, begat those perverted conceptions, Ceremonies, Sayings, which Christians pity or laugh at. Happy are they, which live not in that disadvantage of time, when men could say little for futurity, but from reason. Whereby the noblest mindes fell often upon doubtfull deaths, and melancholly Dissolutions; With these hopes *Socrates* warmed his doubtfull spirits against that cold potion, and *Cato* before he durst give the fatall stroak spent part of the night in reading the immortality of *Plato*, thereby confirming his wavering hand unto the animosity of that attempt.

It is the heaviest stone that melancholy can throw at a man, to tell him he is at the end of his nature; or that there is no further state to come, unto which this seemes progressionall, and otherwise made in vaine; Without this accomplishment the naturall expectation and desire of such a state, were but a fallacy in nature; unsatisfied Considerators would quarrell the justice of their constitutions, and rest content that *Adam* had fallen lower, whereby by knowing no other Originall, and deeper ignorance of themselves, they might have enjoyed the happinesse of inferiour Creatures; who in tranquility possesse their Constitutions, as having not the apprehension to deplore their own natures. And being framed below the circumference of these hopes, or cognition of better being, the wisedom of God hath necessitated their Contentment: But the superiour ingredient and obscured part of our selves, whereto all present felicities afford no resting contentment, will be able at last to tell us we are more than our present selves; and evacuate such hopes in the fruition of their own accomplishments.

CHAPTER V

No w since these dead bones have already out-lasted the living ones of *Methuselah*, and in a yard under ground, and thin walls of clay, out-worn all the strong and specious buildings above it; and quietly rested under the drums and tramplings of three conquests; What Prince can promise such diuturnity unto his Reliques, or might not gladly say,

Sic ego componi versus in ossa velim.

Time which antiquates Antiquities, and hath an art to make dust of all things, hath yet spared these *minor* Monuments. In vain we hope to be known by open and visible conservatories, when to be unknown was the means of their continuation and obscurity their protection: If they dyed by violent hands, and were thrust into their Urnes, these bones become considerable, and some old Philosophers would honour them, whose souls they conceived most pure, which were thus snatched from their bodies; and to retain a stronger propension unto them: whereas they weariedly left a languishing corps, and with faint desires of re-union. If they fell by long and aged decay, yet wrapt up in the bundle of time, they fall into indistinction, and make but one blot with Infants. If we begin to die when we live, and long life be but a prolongation of death, our life is a sad composition; We live with death, and die not in a moment. How many pulses made up the life of *Methuselah*, were work for *Archimedes*: Common Counters summe up the life of *Moses* his man. Our dayes become considerable like petty sums by minute accumulations; where numerous fractions make up but small round numbers; and our dayes of a span long make not one little finger.

If the nearnesse of our last necessity brought a nearer conformity unto it, there were a happinesse in hoary hairs, and

no calamity in half senses. But the long habit of living in-
disposeth us for dying; When Avarice makes us the sport of
death; When even *David* grew politickly cruell; and *Solomon*
could hardly be said to be the wisest of men. But many are
too early old, and before the date of age. Adversity stretcheth
our dayes, misery makes *Alcmenas* nights, and time hath no
wings unto it. But the most tedious being is that which can
unwish it self, content to be nothing, or never to have been,
which was beyond the *male*-content of *Job*, who cursed not
the day of his life, but his Nativity: Content to have so farre
been, as to have a Title to future being; Although he had lived
here but in an hidden state of life, and as it were an abortion.

What Song the *Syrens* sang, or what name *Achilles* assumed
when he hid himself among women, though puzling Questions
are not beyond all conjecture. What time the persons of these
Ossuaries entred the famous Nations of the dead, and slept
with Princes and Counsellours, might admit a wide solution.
But who were the proprietaries of these bones, or what
bodies these ashes made up, were a question above Anti-
quarism. Not to be resolved by man, nor easily perhaps by
spirits, except we consult the Provinciall Guardians, or tutel-
lary Observators. Had they made as good provision for their
names, as they have done for their Reliques, they had not so
grosly erred in the art of perpetuation. But to subsist in
bones, and be but Pyramidally extant, is a fallacy in duration.
Vain ashes, which in the oblivion of names, persons, times, and
sexes, have found unto themselves a fruitlesse continuation,
and only arise unto late posterity, as Emblemes of mortall
vanities; Antidotes against pride, vain-glory, and madding
vices. Pagan vain-glories which thought the world might
last for ever, had encouragement for ambition, and finding no
Atropos unto the immortality of their Names, were never dampt
with the necessity of oblivion. Even old ambitions had the

44

advantage of ours, in the attempts of their vain-glories, who acting early, and before the probable Meridian of time, have by this time found great accomplishment of their designes, whereby the ancient *Heroes* have already out-lasted their Monuments, and Mechanicall preservations. But in this latter Scene of time we cannot expect such Mummies unto our memories, when ambition may fear the Prophecy of *Elias*, and *Charles* the fifth can never hope to live within two *Methusela's* of *Hector*.

And therefore restlesse inquietude for the diuturnity of our memories unto present considerations seems a vanity almost out of date, and superanuated peece of folly. We cannot hope to live so long in our names as some have done in their persons, one face of *Janus* holds no proportion unto the other. 'Tis too late to be ambitious. The great mutations of the world are acted, our time may be too short for our designes. To extend our memories by Monuments, whose death we dayly pray for, and whose duration we cannot hope, without injury to our expectations in the advent of the last day, were a contradiction to our beliefs. We whose generations are ordained in this setting part of time, are providentially taken off from such imaginations. And being necessitated to eye the remaining particle of futurity, are naturally constituted unto thoughts of the next world, and cannot excusably decline the consideration of that duration, which maketh Pyramids pillars of snow, and all that's past a moment.

Circles and right lines limit and close all bodies, and the mortall right-lined circle must conclude and shut up all. There is no antidote against the *Opium* of time, which temporally considereth all things; Our Fathers finde their graves in our short memories, and sadly tell us how we may be buried in our Survivors. Grave-stones tell truth scarce fourty years: Generations passe while some trees stand, and old Families last not three Oaks. To be read by bare Inscriptions like many in *Gruter*, to hope for Eternity by Ænigmaticall Epithetes, or first letters of our names, to be studied by Antiquaries, who we were, and have new Names given us like many of the Mummies, are cold consolations unto the Students of perpetuity, even by everlasting Languages.

To be content that times to come should only know there was such a man, not caring whether they knew more of him, was a frigid ambition in *Cardan*: disparaging his horoscopal inclination and judgement of himself. Who cares to subsist like *Hippocrates* Patients, or *Achilles* horses in *Homer*, under naked nominations, without deserts and noble acts, which are the balsame of our memories, the *Entelechia* and soul of our subsistences? To be namelesse in worthy deeds exceeds an infamous history. The *Canaanitish* woman lives more happily without a name, than *Herodias* with one. And who had not rather have been the good theef, than *Pilate*?

But the iniquity of oblivion blindely scattereth her poppy, and deals with the memory of men without distinction to merit of perpetuity. Who can but pity the founder of the Pyramids? *Herostratus* lives that burnt the Temple of *Diana*, he is almost lost that built it; Time hath spared the Epitaph of *Adrians* horse, confounded that of himself. In vain we compute our felicities by the advantage of our good names, since bad have equall durations; and *Thersites* is like to live as long as *Agamemnon*. Who knows whether the best of men be known? or whether there be not more remarkable persons forgot, than any that stand remembred in the known account of time? Without the favour of the everlasting Register the first man had been as unknown as the last, and *Methuselahs* long life had been his only Chronicle.

Oblivion is not to be hired: The greater part must be content to be as though they had not been, to be found in the

Register of God, not in the record of man. Twenty seven
Names make up the first story, and the recorded names ever
since contain not one living Century. The number of the
dead long exceedeth all that shall live. The night of time far
surpasseth the day, and who knows when was the Æquinox?
Every houre addes unto that current Arithmetique, which
scarce stands one moment. And since death must be the
Lucina of life, and even Pagans could doubt whether thus to
live, were to dye. Since our longest Sunne sets at right
descensions, and makes but winter arches, and therefore it
cannot be long before we lie down in darknesse, and have our
light in ashes. Since the brother of death daily haunts us with
dying *memento's*, and time that grows old it self, bids us hope no
long duration: Diuturnity is a dream and folly of expectation.

Darknesse and light divide the course of time, and oblivion
shares with memory a great part even of our living beings;
we slightly remember our felicities, and the smartest stroaks
of affliction leave but short smart upon us. Sense endureth no
extremities, and sorrows destroy us or themselves. To weep
into stones are fables. Afflictions induce callosities, miseries
are slippery, or fall like snow upon us, which notwithstanding
is no unhappy stupidity. To be ignorant of evils to come, and
forgetfull of evils past, is a mercifull provision in nature,
whereby we digest the mixture of our few and evil dayes, and
our delivered senses not relapsing into cutting remembrances,
our sorrows are not kept raw by the edge of repetitions.
A great part of Antiquity contented their hopes of subsistency
with a transmigration of their souls. A good way to continue
their memories, while having the advantage of plurall suc-
cessions, they could not but act something remarkable in
such variety of beings, and enjoying the fame of their passed
selves, make accumulation of glory unto their last durations.
Others rather than be lost in the uncomfortable night of

nothing, were content to recede into the common being, and make one particle of the publick soul of all things, which was no more than to return into their unknown and divine Originall again. Ægyptian ingenuity was more unsatisfied, continuing their bodies in sweet consistences, to attend the return of their souls. But all was vanity, feeding the winde, and folly. The Ægyptian Mummies, which *Cambyses* or time hath spared, avarice now consumeth. Mummie is become Merchandise, *Misʒraim* cures wounds, and *Pharaoh* is sold for balsoms.

In vain do individuals hope for Immortality, or any patent from oblivion, in preservations below the Moon: Men have been deceived even in their flatteries above the Sun, and studied conceits to perpetuate their names in heaven. The various Cosmography of that part hath already varied the names of contrived constellations; *Nimrod* is lost in *Orion*, and *Osyris* in the Dogge-starre. While we look for incorruption in the heavens, we finde they are but like the Earth; Durable in their main bodies, alterable in their parts: whereof beside Comets and new Stars, perspectives begin to tell tales. And the spots that wander about the Sun, with *Phaetons* favour, would make clear conviction.

There is nothing strictly immortall, but immortality. Whatever hath no beginning may be confident of no end (all others have a dependent being, and within the reach of destruction) which is the peculiar of that necessary essence that cannot destroy it self; And the highest strain of omnipotency to be so powerfully constituted, as not to suffer even from the power of it self. But the sufficiency of Christian Immortality frustrates all earthly glory, and the quality of either state after death makes a folly of posthumous memory. God who only can destroy our souls, and hath assured our resurrection, either of our bodies or names hath directly promised no duration. Wherein there is so much of chance that the boldest

Expectants have found unhappy frustration; and to hold long subsistence, seems but a scape in oblivion. But man is a Noble Animal, splendid in ashes, and pompous in the grave, solemnizing Nativities and Deaths with equall lustre, nor omitting Ceremonies of bravery, in the infamy of his nature.

Life is a pure flame, and we live by an invisible Sun within us. A small fire sufficeth for life, great flames seemed too little after death, while men vainly affected precious pyres, and to burn like *Sardanapalus*; but the wisedom of funerall Laws found the folly of prodigall blazes, and reduced undoing fires unto the rule of sober obsequies, wherein few could be so mean as not to provide wood, pitch, a mourner, and an Urne.

Five languages secured not the Epitaph of *Gordianus*; The man of God lives longer without a Tomb than any by one, invisibly interred by Angels, and adjudged to obscurity though not without some marks directing human discovery. *Enoch* and *Elias* without either tomb or buriall, in an anomalous state of being, are the great Examples of perpetuity in their long and living memory, in strict account being still on this side death, and having a late part yet to act upon this stage of earth. If in the decretory term of the world we shall not all dye but be changed, according to received translation, the last day will make but few graves; at least quick Resurrections will anticipate lasting Sepultures; Some Graves will be opened before they be quite closed, and *Laʒarus* be no wonder. When many that feared to dye shall groane that they can dye but once, the dismall state is the second and living death; when life puts despair on the damned; when men shall wish the coverings of Mountaines, not of Monuments, and annihilation shall be courted.

While some have studied Monuments, others have studiously declined them: and some have been so vainly boisterous, that they durst not acknowledge their Graves; wherein

Alaricus seems most subtle, who had a River turned to hide his bones at the bottome. Even *Sylla* that thought himself safe in his Urne, could not prevent revenging tongues, and stones thrown at his Monument. Happy are they whom privacy makes innocent, who deal so with men in this world, that they are not afraid to meet them in the next, who when they dye, make no commotion among the dead, and are not toucht with that poeticall taunt of *Isaiah.*

Pyramids, Arches, Obelisks, were but the irregularities of vain-glory, and wilde enormities of ancient magnanimity. But the most magnanimous resolution rests in the Christian Religion, which trampleth upon pride, and sits on the neck of ambition, humbly pursuing that infallible perpetuity, unto which all others must diminish their diameters, and be poorly seen in Angles of contingency.

Pious spirits who passed their dayes in raptures of futurity, made little more of this world than the world that was before it, while they lay obscure in the Chaos of pre-ordination, and night of their fore-beings. And if any have been so happy as truly to understand Christian annihilation, extasis, exolution, liquefaction, transformation, the kisse of the Spouse, gustation of God, and ingression into the divine shadow, they have already had an handsome anticipation of heaven; the glory of the world is surely over, and the earth in ashes unto them.

To subsist in lasting Monuments, to live in their productions, to exist in their names, and prædicament of *Chymera's,* was large satisfaction unto old expectations, and made one part of their *Elyʒiums.* But all this is nothing in the Metaphysicks of true belief. To live indeed is to be again our selves, which being not only an hope but an evidence in noble beleevers, 'Tis all one to lye in St *Innocents* Church-yard, as in the Sands of *Ægypt*: Ready to be any thing, in the extasie of being ever, and as content with six foot as the Moles of *Adrianus.*

THE GARDEN OF CYRUS

OR

THE QUINCUNCIALL, LOZENGE OR NET-WORK
PLANTATIONS OF THE ANCIENTS,
ARTIFICIALLY, NATURALLY, MYSTICALLY
CONSIDERED

*Had I not observed that Purblinde men have discoursed well of
sight, and some without issue, excellently of Generation; I that
was never master of any considerable garden, had not attempted
this Subject. But the Earth is the Garden of Nature, and each
fruitfull Countrey a Paradise.* Dioscorides *made most of his
Observations in his march about with* Antonius; *and* Theophrastus *raised his generalities chiefly from the field.*

*Beside we write no Herball, nor can this Volume deceive you,
who have handled the massiest thereof: who know that three
Folio's are yet too little, and how New Herbals fly from* America
*upon us. From persevering Enquirers, and old in those singu-
larities, we expect such Descriptions. Wherein* England *is now
so exact, that it yeelds not to other Countreys.*

*We pretend not to multiply vegetable divisions by Quincuncial
and Reticulate plants; or erect a new Phytology. The Field of
knowledge hath been so traced, it is hard to spring any thing new.
Of old things we write something new, If truth may receive
addition, or envy will have any thing new; since the Ancients
knew the late Anatomicall discoveries, and* Hippocrates *the
Circulation.*

*You have been so long out of trite learning, that 'tis hard to
finde a subject proper for you; and if you have met with a Sheet
upon this, we have missed our intention. In this multiplicity of
writing, bye and barren Themes are best fitted for invention;
Subjects so often discoursed confine the Imagination, and fix
our conceptions unto the notions of fore-writers. Beside, such*

Discourses allow excursions, and venially admit of collaterall truths, though at some distance from their principals. Wherein if we sometimes take wide liberty, we are not single, but erre by great example.

He that will illustrate the excellency of this order, may easily fail upon so spruce a Subject, wherein we have not affrighted the common Reader with any other Diagramms than of it self; and have industriously declined illustrations from rare and unknown plants.

Your discerning judgement so well acquainted with that study, will expect herein no mathematicall truths, as well understanding how few generalities and U *finita's there are in nature. How* Scaliger *hath found exceptions in most Universals of* Aristotle *and* Theophrastus. *How Botanicall Maximes must have fair allowance, and are tolerably currant, if not intolerably overballanced by exceptions.*

You have wisely ordered your vegetable delights, beyond the reach of exception. The Turks who passt their dayes in Gardens here, will have Gardens also hereafter, and delighting in Flowers on earth, must have Lillies and Roses in Heaven. In Garden Delights 'tis not easie to hold a Mediocrity; that insinuating pleasure is seldome without some extremity. The Antients venially delighted in flourishing Gardens; Many were Florists that knew not the true use of a Flower; And in Plinies *dayes none had directly treated of that Subject. Some commendably affected Plantations of venemous Vegetables, some confined their delights unto single plants, and* Cato *seemed to dote upon Cabbadge; While the Ingenuous delight of Tulipists stands saluted with hard language, even by their own Professors.*

That in this Garden Discourse we range into extraneous things, and many parts of Art and Nature, we follow herein the example of old and new Plantations, wherein noble spirits contented not themselves with Trees, but by the attendance of

Aviaries, Fish Ponds, and all variety of Animals, they made their gardens the Epitome of the earth, and some resemblance of the secular shows of old.

That we conjoyn these parts of different Subjects, or that this should succeed the other; Your judgement will admit without impute of incongruity; Since the delightfull World comes after death, and Paradise succeeds the Grave. Since the verdant state of things is the Symbole of the Resurrection, and to flourish in the state of Glory, we must first be sown in corruption. Beside the ancient practise of Noble Persons, to conclude in Garden-Graves, and Urnes themselves of old, to be wrapt up in flowers and garlands.

Nullum sine venia placuisse eloquium, *is more sensibly understood by Writers than by Readers; nor well apprehended by either, till works have hanged out like* Apelles *his Pictures; wherein even common eyes will finde something for emendation.*

To wish all Readers of your abilities, were unreasonably to multiply the number of Scholars beyond the temper of these times. But unto this ill-judging age, we charitably desire a portion of your equity, judgement, candour, and ingenuity; wherein you are so rich, as not to lose by diffusion. And being a flourishing branch of that Noble Family, unto which we owe so much ob-servance, you are not new set, but long rooted in such perfection; whereof having had so lasting confirmation in your worthy conversation, constant amity, and expression; and knowing you a serious Student in the highest arcana's *of Nature; with much excuse we bring these low delights, and poor maniples to your Treasure.*

Your affectionate Friend

and Servant,

Thomas Browne.

Norwich

May 1

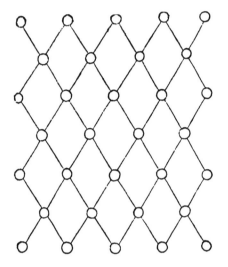

Quid Quincunce speciosius, qui, in quam cunqʒ partem spectaueris, rectus est. Quintilian:ⁿ

THE GARDEN OF CYRUS

CHAPTER I

THAT *Vulcan* gave arrows unto *Apollo* and *Diana* the fourth day after their Nativities, according to Gentile Theology, may passe for no blinde apprehension of the Creation of the Sunne and Moon, in the work of the fourth day; When the diffused light contracted into Orbes, and shooting rayes, of those Luminaries. Plainer Descriptions there are from Pagan pens, of the creatures of the fourth day; While the divine Philosopher unhappily omitteth the noblest part of the third; And *Ovid* (whom many conceive to have borrowed his description from *Moses*) coldly deserting the remarkable account of the text, in three words, describeth this work of the third day; the vegetable creation, and first ornamentall Scene of nature; the primitive food of animals, and first story of Physick, in Dietetical conservation.

For though Physick may pleade high, from that medicall act of God, in casting so deep a sleep upon our first Parent; And Chirurgery finde its whole art, in that one passage concerning the Rib of *Adam*, yet is there no rivality with Garden contrivance and Herbery. For if Paradise were planted the third day of the Creation, as wiser Divinity concludeth, the Nativity thereof was too early for Horoscopie; Gardens were before Gardiners, and but some hours after the earth.

Of deeper doubt is its Topography, and locall designation; yet being the primitive garden, and without much controversie seated in the East, it is more than probable the first curiosity, and cultivation of plants, most flourished in those quarters. And since the Ark of *Noah* first toucht upon some mountains of *Armenia*, the planting art arose again in the East, and found its revolution not far from the place of its Nativity, about the Plains of those Regions. And if *Zoroaster* were either *Cham*, *Chus*, or *Mizraim*, they were early proficients therein, who left (as *Pliny* delivereth) a work of Agriculture.

However the account of the Pensill or hanging gardens of *Babylon*, if made by *Semiramis*, the third or fourth from *Nimrod*, is of no slender antiquity; which being not framed upon ordinary levell of ground, but raised upon pillars, admitting under-passages, we cannot accept as the first *Babylonian* Gardens; But a more eminent progress and advancement in that art, than any that went before it: Somewhat answering or hinting the old Opinion concerning Paradise it self, with many conceptions elevated above the plane of the Earth.

Nebuchodonosor whom some will have to be the famous *Syrian* King of *Diodorus*, beautifully repaired that City; and so magnificently built his hanging gardens, that from succeeding Writers he had the honour of the first. From whence over-looking *Babylon*, and all the Region about it, he found no circumscription to the eye of his ambition; till over-delighted with the bravery of this Paradise, in his melancholy metamorphosis, he found the folly of that delight, and a proper punishment, in the contrary habitation, in wilde plantations and wandrings of the fields.

The *Persian* Gallants who destroyed this Monarchy, maintained their Botanicall bravery. Unto whom we owe the very name of Paradise: wherewith we meet not in Scripture before the time of *Solomon*, and conceived originally *Persian*. The word for that disputed Garden expressing in the Hebrew no more than a Field enclosed, which from the same Root is content to derive a garden and a Buckler.

Cyrus the elder, brought up in Woods and Mountains,

when time and power enabled, pursued the dictate of his education, and brought the treasures of the field into rule and circum-scription. So nobly beautifying the hanging Gardens of *Babylon*, that he was also thought to be the authour thereof.

Ahasuerus (whom many conceive to have been *Artaxerxes Longimanus*) in the Countrey and City of Flowers, and in an open Garden, entertained his Princes and people, while *Vasthi* more modestly treated the Ladies within the Palace thereof.

But if (as some opinion) King *Ahasuerus* were *Artaxerxes Mnemon*, that found a life and reign answerable unto his great memory, our magnified *Cyrus* was his second Brother: who gave the occasion of that memorable work, and almost miraculous retrait of *Xenophon*. A person of high spirit and honour, naturally a King, though fatally prevented by the harmlesse chance of *post*-geniture: Not only a Lord of Gardens, but a manuall planter thereof: disposing his trees like his armies in regular ordination. So that while old *Laertas* hath found a name in *Homer* for pruning hedges, and clearing away thorns and bryars; while King *Attalus* lives for his poysonous plantations of *Aconites*, Henbane, Hellebore, and plants hardly admitted within the walls of Paradise; While many of the Ancients do poorly live in the single name of Vegetables; All stories do look upon *Cyrus*, as the splendid and regular planter.

According whereto *Xenophon* describeth his gallant plantation at *Sardis*, thus rendred by *Strebæus*. *Arbores pari intervallo sitas, rectos ordines, & omnia perpulchrè in Quincuncem directa.* Which we shall take for granted as being accordingly rendred by the most elegant of the *Latines*; and by no made term, but in use before by *Varro*. That is the rows and orders so handsomly disposed; or five trees so set together, that a regular angularity, and through prospect, was left on every side. Owing this name not only unto the Quintuple number of Trees, but the figure declaring that number; which being doubled at the angle, makes up the Letter χ, that is the Emphaticall decussation, or fundamentall figure.

Now though in some ancient and modern practice the *area* or decussated plot, might be a perfect square, answerable to a *Tuscan Pedestall,* and the *Quinquernio* or Cinque-point of a dye; wherein by Diagonall lines the intersection was rect-angular; accomodable unto Plantations of large growing Trees; and we must not deny our selves the advantage of this order; yet shall we chiefly insist upon that of *Curtius* and *Porta,* in their brief description hereof. Wherein the *decussis* is made within a longilaterall square, with opposite angles, acute and obtuse at the intersection; and so upon progression making a *Rhombus* or Lozenge figuration, which seemeth very agreeable unto the Originall figure; Answerable whereunto we observe the decussated characters in many consulary Coynes, and even in those of *Constantine* and his Sons, which pretend their pattern in the Sky; the crucigerous Ensigne carried this figure, not transversely or rectangularly inter-sected, but in a decussation, after the form of an *Andrean* or *Burgundian* cross, which answereth this description.

Where by the way we shall decline the old Theme, so traced by antiquity, of crosses and crucifixion: Whereof some being right, and of one single peece without transversion or transome, do little advantage our subject. Nor shall we take in the mysticall *Tau,* or the Crosse of our blessed Saviour, which having in some descriptions an *Empedon* or crossing foot-stay, made not one single transversion. And since the Learned *Lipsius* hath made some doubt even of the Crosse of St *Andrew,* since some Martyrologicall Histories deliver his death by the generall Name of a crosse, and *Hippolitus* will have him suffer by the sword; we should have enough to make out the received Crosse of that Martyr. Nor shall we urge the *labarum,* and famous Standard of *Constantine,* or

make further use thereof, than as the first Letters in the Name
of our Saviour Christ, in use among Christians before the
dayes of *Constantine*, to be observed in Sepulchral Monuments
of Martyrs, in the Reign of *Adrian*, and *Antoninus*; and to be
found in the Antiquities of the Gentiles, before the advent of
Christ, as in the Medall of King *Ptolemy*, signed with the
same characters, and might be the beginning of some word
or name, which Antiquaries have not hit on.

We will not revive the mysterious crosses of *Ægypt*, with
circles on their heads, in the breast of *Serapis*, and the hands
of their Geniall spirits, not unlike the character of *Venus*, and
looked on by ancient Christians, with relation unto Christ.
Since however they first began, the Ægyptians thereby
expressed the processe and motion of the spirit of the world,
and the diffusion thereof upon the Celestiall and Elementall
nature; implyed by a circle and right-lined intersection.
A secret in their Telesmes and magicall Characters among
them. Though he that considereth the plain crosse upon the
head of the Owl in the Laterane Obelisk, or the crosse erected
upon a picher diffusing streams of water into two basins, with
sprinkling branches in them, and all described upon a two-
footed Altar, as in the Hieroglyphicks of the brasen Table
of *Bembus*; will hardly decline all thought of Christian signality
in them.

We shall not call in the Hebrew *Tenupha*, or ceremony of
their Oblations, waved by the Priest unto the four quarters
of the world, after the form of a cross; as in the peace-offerings.
And if it were clearly made out what is remarkably delivered
from the Traditions of the Rabbins, that as the Oyle was
powred coronally or circularly upon the head of Kings, so the
High-Priest was anointed decussatively or in the form of a X;
though it could not escape a typicall thought of Christ, from
mysticall considerators; yet being the conceit is Hebrew, we

should rather expect its verification from Analogy in that language, than to confine the same unto the unconcerned Letters of *Greece*, or make it out by the characters of *Cadmus* or *Palamedes*.

Of this Quincunciall Ordination the Ancients practised much, discoursed little; and the Moderns have nothing enlarged; which he that more nearly considereth, in the form of its square *Rhombus*, and decussation, with the severall commodities, mysteries, parallelismes, and resemblances, both in Art and Nature, shall easily discern the elegancy of this order.

That this was in some wayes of practice in diverse and distant Nations, hints or deliveries there are from no slender Antiquity. In the hanging Gardens of *Babylon*, from *Abydenus*, *Eusebius*, and others, *Curtius* describeth this Rule of decussation. In the memorable Garden of *Alcinous*, anciently conceived an originall phancy, from Paradise, mention there is of well contrived order; For so hath *Didymus* and *Eustathius* expounded the emphatical word. *Diomedes* describing the Rurall possessions of his father, gives account in the same Language of Trees orderly planted. And *Ulysses* being a boy was promised by his Father fourty Figge-trees, and fifty rows of Vines producing all kinde of grapes.

That the Eastern Inhabitants of *India* made use of such order, even in open Plantations, is deducible from *Theophrastus*; who describing the trees whereof they made their garments, plainly delivereth that they were planted κατ'ὄρχους, and in such order that at a distance men would mistake them for Vineyards. The same seems confirmed in *Greece* from a singular expression in *Aristotle* concerning the order of Vines, delivered by a military term representing the orders of Souldiers, which also confirmeth the antiquity of this form yet used in vineall plantations.

That the same was used in Latine plantations is plainly

confirmed from the commending penne of *Varro*, *Quintilian*, and handsome Description of *Virgil*.

That the first Plantations not long after the Floud were disposed after this manner, the generality and antiquity of this order observed in Vineyards, and Wine plantations, affordeth some conjecture. And since from judicious enquiry, *Saturn* who divided the world between his three sonnes, who beareth a Sickle in his hand, who taught the plantations of Vines, the setting, grafting of trees, and the best part of Agriculture, is discovered to be *Noah*, whether this early dispersed Husbandry in Vineyards had not its Originall in that Patriarch, is no such Paralogicall doubt.

And if it were clear that this was used by *Noah* after the Floud, I could easily beleeve it was in use before it; Not willing to fix to such ancient inventions no higher originall than *Noah*; Nor readily conceiving those aged *Heroes*, whose diet was vegetable, and only or chiefly consisted in the fruits of the earth, were much deficient in their splendid cultivations; or after the experience of fifteen hundred years, left much for future discovery in Botanicall Agriculture. Nor fully perswaded that Wine was the invention of *Noah*, that fermented Liquors, which often make themselves, so long escaped their Luxury or experience; that the first sinne of the new world was no sin of the old. That *Cain* and *Abel* were the first that offered Sacrifice; or because the Scripture is silent that *Adam* or *Isaac* offered none at all.

Whether *Abraham*, brought up in the first planting Countrey, observed not some rule hereof, when he planted a grove at *Beer-sheba*; or whether at least a like ordination were not in the Garden of *Solomon*, probability may contest. Answerably unto the wisedom of that eminent Botanologer, and orderly disposer of all his other works. Especially since this was one peece of Gallantry, wherein he pursued the specious part of felicity, according to his own description. I made me Gardens and Orchards, and planted Trees in them of all kindes of fruit. I made me Pools of water, to water therewith the wood that bringeth forth Trees; which was no ordinary plantation, if according to the *Targum*, or *Chaldee Paraphrase*, it contained all kindes of Plants, and some fetched as far as *India*; And the extent thereof were from the wall of *Jerusalem* unto the water of *Siloah*.

And if *Jordan* were but *Jaar Eden*, that is, the River of *Eden*, *Genesar* but *Gansar* or the Prince of Gardens; and it could be made out, that the Plain of *Jordan* were watered not comparatively, but causally, and because it was the Paradise of God, as the Learned *Abramas* hinteth, he was not far from the Prototype and originall of Plantations. And since even in Paradise it self, the tree of knowledge was placed in the middle of the Garden, whatever was the ambient figure, there wanted not a centre and rule of decussation. Whether the groves and sacred Plantations of Antiquity were not thus orderly placed, either by *quaternio's*, or quintuple ordinations, may favourably be doubted. For since they were so methodicall in the constitutions of their temples, as to observe the due situation, aspect, manner, form, and order in Architectonicall relations, whether they were not as distinct in their groves and Plantations about them, in form and *species* respectively unto their Deities, is not without probability of conjecture. And in their groves of the Sunne this was a fit number, by multiplication to denote the dayes of the year; and might Hieroglyphically speak as much, as the mysticall *Statua* of *Janus* in the Language of his fingers. And since they were so criticall in the number of his horses, the strings of his Harp, and rayes about his head, denoting the orbes of heaven, the Seasons and Moneths of the Yeare; witty Idolatry would hardly be flat in other appropriations.

CHAPTER II

NOR was this only a form of practise in Plantations, but found imitation from high Antiquity, in sundry artificiall contrivances and manuall operations. For to omit the position of squared stones, *cuneatim* or *wedgwise* in the Walls of *Roman* and *Gothick* buildings; and the *lithostrata* or figured pavements of the ancients, which consisted not all of square stones, but were divided into triquetrous segments, honey-combs, and sexangular figures, according to *Vitruvius*; The squared stones and bricks in ancient fabricks were placed after this order. And two above or below conjoyned by a middle stone or *Plinthus*, observable in the ruines of *Forum Nervæ*, the *Mausoleum* of *Augustus*, the Pyramid of *Cestius*, and the sculpture draughts of the larger Pyramids of Ægypt. And therefore in the draughts of eminent fabricks, Painters do commonly imitate this order in the lines of their description.

In the Laureat draughts of sculpture and picture, the leaves and foliate works are commonly thus contrived, which is but in imitation of the *Pulvinaria*, and ancient pillow-work, observable in *Ionick* peeces, about columns, temples and altars. To omit many other analogies, in Architectonicall draughts, which art it self is founded upon fives, as having its subject, and most gracefull peeces divided by this number.

The Triumphal Oval, and Civicall Crowns of Laurel, Oake, and Myrtle, when fully made, were pleated after this order. And to omit the crossed Crowns of Christian Princes; what figure that was which *Anastatius* described upon the head of *Leo* the third; or who first brought in the Arched Crown; That of Charles the great, (which seems the first remarkably closed Crown,) was framed after this manner; with an intersection in the middle from the main crossing barres, and the interspaces unto the frontal circle, continued by handsome network-plates, much after this order. Whereon we shall not insist, because from greater Antiquity, and practice of consecration, we meet with the radiated, and starry Crown, upon the head of *Augustus*, and many succeeding Emperors. Since the Armenians and Parthians had a peculiar royall Capp; And the Grecians from *Alexander* another kinde of diadem. And even Diadems themselves were but fasciations, and handsome ligatures, about the heads of Princes; nor wholly omitted in the mitrall Crown, which common picture seems to set too upright and forward upon the head of *Aaron*: Worne sometimes singly, or doubly by Princes, according to their Kingdomes; and no more to be expected from two Crowns at once, upon the head of *Ptolemy*. And so easily made out when historians tell us, some bound up wounds, some hanged themselves with diadems.

The beds of the antients were corded somewhat after this fashion: That is not directly, as ours at present, but obliquely, from side to side, and after the manner of network; whereby they strengthened the spondæ or bedsides, and spent less cord in the work: as is demonstrated by *Blancanus*.

And as they lay in crossed beds, so they sat upon seeming crosselegg'd seats: in which form the noblest thereof were framed: Observable in the triumphall seats, the *sella curulis*, or *Ædyle Chayres*, in the coyns of *Cestius*, *Sylla*, and *Julius*. That they sat also crosse legg'd many noble draughts declare; and in this figure the sitting gods and goddesses are drawn in medalls and medallions. And beside this kinde of work in Retiarie and hanging textures, in embroderies, and eminent needle-works; the like is obvious unto every eye in glass-windows. Nor only in Glassie contrivances, but also in Lattice and Stone-work, conceived in the Temple of *Solomon*; wherein the windows are termed *fenestræ reticulatæ*, or lights

framed like nets. And agreeable unto the Greek expression
concerning Christ in the Canticles, looking through the nets
which ours hath rendered, he looketh forth at the windows,
shewing himselfe through the lattesse; that is, partly seen
and unseen, according to the visible and invisible side of his
nature. To omit the noble reticulate work, in the chapiters of
the pillars of *Solomon*, with Lillies, and Pomegranats upon
a network ground; and the *Craticula* or grate through which
the ashes fell in the altar of burnt offerings.

That the networks and nets of antiquity were little different
in the form from ours at present, is confirmable from the nets
in the hands of the Retiarie gladiators, the proper combatants
with the secutores. To omit the ancient Conopeion or gnatnet
of the Ægyptians, the inventors of that Artifice: the rushey
labyrinths of *Theocritus*; the nosegaynets, which hung from
the head under the nostrils of Princes; and that uneasie
metaphor of *Reticulum Jecoris*, which some expound the lobe,
we the caule above the liver. As for that famous network of
Vulcan, which inclosed *Mars* and *Venus*, and caused that
unextinguishable laugh in heaven; since the gods themselves
could not discern it, we shall not prie into it; Although why
Vulcan bound them, *Neptune* loosed them, and *Apollo* should
first discover them, might afford no vulgar mythologie.
Heralds have not omitted this order or imitation thereof,
whiles they Symbollically adorn their Scuchions with Mascles
Fusils and Saltyrs, and while they disposed the figures of
Ermins and vaired coats in this Quincuncial method.

The same is not forgot by Lapidaries while they cut their
gemms pyramidally, or by æquicrural triangles. Perspective
picturers, in their Base, Horison, and lines of distances, cannot
escape these Rhomboidall decussations. Sculptors in their
strongest shadows, after this order do draw their double
Haches. And the very *Americans* do naturally fall upon it,

in their neat and curious textures, which is also observed in the elegant artifices of *Europe*. But this is no law unto the woof of the neat *Retiarie* Spider, which seems to weave without transversion, and by the union of right lines to make out a continued surface, which is beyond the common art of Textury, and may still nettle *Minerva* the Goddesse of that mystery. And he that shall hatch the little seeds, either found in small webs, or white round Egges, carried under the bellies of some Spiders, and behold how at their first production in boxes, they will presently fill the same with their webbs, may observe the early and untaught finger of nature, and how they are natively provided with a stock, sufficient for such Texture.

The Rurall charm against *Dodder, Tetter*, and strangling weeds, was contrived after this order, while they placed a chalked Tile at the four corners, and one in the middle of their fields, which though ridiculous in the intention, was rationall in the contrivance, and a good way to diffuse the magick through all parts of the *Area*.

Somewhat after this manner they ordered the little stones in the old game of *Pentalithismus*, or casting up five stones to catch them on the back of their hand. And with some resemblance hereof, the *Proci* or Prodigall Paramours disposed their men, when they played at *Penelope*. For being themselves an hundred and eight, they set fifty four stones on either side, and one in the middle, which they called *Penelope*, which he that hit was master of the game.

In Chesse-boards and Tables we yet finde Pyramids and Squares, I wish we had their true and ancient description, farre different from ours, or the *Chet mat* of the *Persians*, which might continue some elegant remarkables, as being an invention as High as *Hermes* the Secretary of *Osyris*, figuring the whole world, the motion of the Planets, with Eclipses of Sunne and Moon.

Physicians are not without the use of this decussation in several operations, in ligatures and union of dissolved continuities. Mechanicks make use hereof in forcipall Organs, and Instruments of Incision; wherein who can but magnifie the power of decussation, inservient to contrary ends, solution and consolidation, union, and divisions, illustrable from *Aristotle* in the old *Nucifragium* or Nut-cracker, and the Instruments of Evulsion, compression or incision; which consisting of two *Vectes* or armes, converted towards each other, the innitency and stresse being made upon the *hypomochlion* or fulciment in the decussation, the greater compression is made by the union of two impulsors.

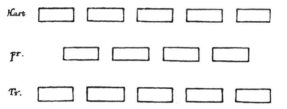

The *Roman Batalia* was ordered after this manner, whereof as sufficiently known *Virgil* hath left but an hint, and obscure intimation. For thus were the maniples and cohorts of the *Hastati*, *Principes* and *Triarii* placed in their bodies, wherein consisted the strength of the *Roman* battle. By this Ordination they readily fell into each other; the *Hastati* being pressed, handsomely retired into the intervalls of the *principes*, these into that of the *Triarii*, which making as it were a new body, might joyntly renew the battle, wherein consisted the secret of their successes. And therefore it was remarkably singular in the battle of *Africa*, that *Scipio* fearing a rout from the Elephants of the Enemy, left not the *Principes* in their alternate distances, whereby the Elephants passing the vacuities of the *Hastati*, might have run upon them, but drew his battle into right order, and leaving the passages bare, defeated the mischief intended by the Elephants. Out of this figure were made two remarkable forms of Battle, the *Cuneus* and *Forceps*, or the sheare and wedge battles, each made of half a *Rhombus*, and but differenced by position. The wedge invented to break or work into a body, the *forceps* to environ and defeat the power thereof, composed out of the selectest Souldiery and disposed into the form of an U, wherein receiving the wedge, it inclosed it on both sides. After this form the famous *Narses* ordered his battle against the *Franks*, and by this figure the *Almans* were enclosed, and cut in peeces.

The *Rhombus* or Lozenge figure so visible in this order, was also a remarkable form of battle in the *Grecian* Cavalry, observed by the *Thessalians*, and *Philip* King of *Macedon*, and frequently by the *Parthians*, As being most ready to turn every way, and best to be commanded, as having its ductors, or Commanders at each Angle.

The *Macedonian Phalanx* (a long time thought invincible) consisted of a long square. For though they might be sixteen in Rank and file, yet when they shut close, so that the sixt pike advanced before the first ranck, though the number might be square, the figure was oblong, answerable unto the Quincunciall quadrate of *Curtius*. According to this square, *Thucydides* delivers, the *Athenians* disposed their battle against the *Lacedemonians* brickwise, and by the same word the Learned *Guellius* expoundeth the quadrate of *Virgil*, after the form of a brick or tile.

And as the first station and position of trees, so was the first habitation of men, not in round Cities, as of later foundation; For the form of *Babylon* the first City was square, and so shall also be the last, according to the description of the holy City in the Apocalyps. The famous pillars of *Seth* before the floud, had also the like foundation, if they were but *anti-*

diluvian Obelisks, and such as *Cham* and his *Ægyptian* race imitated after the Floud.

But *Nineveh* which Authours acknowledge to have exceeded *Babylon*, was of a longilaterall figure, ninety five Furlongs broad, and an hundred and fifty long, and so making about sixty miles in circuit, which is the measure of three dayes journey, according unto military marches, or castrensiall mansions. So that if *Jonas* entred at the narrower side, he found enough for one dayes walk to attain the heart of the City, to make his Proclamation. And if we imagine a City extending from *Ware* to *London*, the expression will be moderate of six score thousand Infants, although we allow vacuities, fields, and intervals of habitation as there needs must be when the monument of *Ninus* took up no lesse than ten furlongs.

And, though none of the seven wonders, yet a noble peece of Antiquity, and made by a Copy exceeding all the rest, had its principall parts disposed after this manner, that is, the Labyrinth of *Crete*, built upon a long quadrate, containing five large squares, communicating by right inflections, terminating in the centre of the middle square, and lodging of the *Minotaur*, if we conform unto the description of the elegant medall thereof in *Agostino*. And though in many accounts we reckon grosly by the square, yet is that very often to be accepted as a long sided quadrate, which was the figure of the Ark of the Covenant, the table of the Shew-bread, and the stone wherein the names of the twelve Tribes were engraved, that is, three in a row, naturally making a longilaterall Figure, the perfect quadrate being made by nine.

What figure the stones themselves maintained, tradition and Scripture are silent, yet Lapidaries in precious stones affect a Table or long square, and in such proportion, that the two laterall and also the three inferiour Tables are equall unto the superiour, and the angles of the laterall Tables contain and constitute the *hypothenusæ*, or broader sides subtending.

That the Tables of the Law were of this figure, general imitation and tradition hath confirmed; yet are we unwilling to load the shoulders of *Moses* with such massie stones, as some pictures lay upon them, since 'tis plainly delivered that he came down with them in his hand; since the word strictly taken implies no such massie hewing, but cutting, and fashioning of them into shape and surface; since some will have them Emeralds, and if they were made of the materials of Mount *Sina*, not improbable that they were marble: Since the words were not many, the letters short of seven hundred, and the Tables written on both sides required no such capacity.

The beds of the Ancients were different from ours at present, which are almost square, being framed ob-long, and about a double unto their breadth; not much unlike the *area*, or bed of this Quincuncial quadrate. The single beds of *Greece* were six foot, and a little more in length, three in breadth; the Giant-like bed of *Og*, which had four cubits of bredth, nine and a half in length, varied not much from this proportion. The Funeral bed of King *Cheops*, in the greater Pyramid, which holds seven in length, and four foot in bredth, had no great difformity from this measure; And whatsoever were the bredth, the length could hardly be lesse, of the tyrannical bed of *Procrustes*, since in a shorter measure he had not been fitted with persons for his cruelty of extension. But the old sepulchral bed, or *Amazonian* Tomb in the market-place of *Megara*, was in the form of a Lozenge; readily made out by the composure of the body. For the arms not lying fasciated or wrapt up after the *Grecian* manner, but in a middle distention, the including lines will strictly make out that figure.

72

CHAPTER III

N o w although this elegant ordination of vegetables hath found coincidence or imitation in sundry works of Art, yet is it not also destitute of naturall examples, and though overlooked by all, was elegantly observable in severall works of nature.

Could we satisfie our selves in the position of the lights above, or discover the wisedom of that order so invariably maintained in the fixed Stars of heaven; Could we have any light, why the stellary part of the first masse, separated into this order, that the Girdle of *Orion* should ever maintain its line, and the two Starres in *Charles's* Wain never leave pointing at the Pole-Starre, we might abate the *Pythagoricall* Musick of the Spheres, the sevenfold Pipe of *Pan*; and the strange Cryptography of *Gaffarell* in his Starrie Booke of Heaven.

But not to look so high as Heaven or the single Quincunx of the *Hyades* upon the head of *Taurus*, the Triangle and remarkable *Crusero* about the foot of the *Centaur*; observable rudiments there are hereof in subterraneous concretions, and bodies in the Earth; in the *Gypsum* or *Talcum Rhomboides*, in the Favaginites or honey-comb-stone, in the *Asteria* and *Astroites*, and in the crucigerous stone of S. *Iago* of *Gallicia*.

The same is observably effected in the *Julus*, *Catkins*, or pendulous excrescencies of severall Trees, of Wallnuts, Alders, and Hazels, which hanging all the Winter, and maintaining their Net-worke close, by the expansion thereof are the early foretellers of the Spring, discoverable also in long Pepper, and elegantly in the *Julus* of *Calamus Aromaticus*, so plentifully growing with us in the first palmes of Willowes, and in the Flowers of Sycamore, Petasites, Asphodelus, and *Blattaria*, before explication. After such order stand the flowery Branches in our best spread *Verbascum*, and the seeds about the spicous head or torch of *Tapsus Barbatus*, in as fair a regularity as the circular and wreathed order will admit, which advanceth one side of the square, and makes the same Rhomboidall.

In the squamous heads of *Scabious*, *Knapweed*, and the elegant *Jacea Pinea*, and in the Scaly composure of the *Oak-Rose*, which some years most aboundeth. After this order hath Nature planted the Leaves in the Head of the common and prickled Artichoak; wherein the black and shining Flies do shelter themselves, when they retire from the purple Flower about it; The same is also found in the pricks, sockets, and impressions of the seeds, in the pulp or bottome thereof; wherein do elegantly stick the Fathers of their Mother. To omit the Quincunciall Specks on the top of the Miscle-berry, especially that which grows upon the *Tilia* or Lime-Tree. And the remarkable disposure of those yellow fringes about the purple Pestill of *Aaron*, and elegant clusters of Dragons, so peculiarly secured by nature, with an *umbrella* or skreening Leaf about them.

The Spongy leaves of some Sea-wracks, Fucus, Oaks, in their severall kindes, found about the shoar, with ejectments of the Sea, are over-wrought with Net-work elegantly containing this order, which plainly declareth the naturality of this texture; And how the needle of nature delighteth to work, even in low and doubtful vegetations.

The *Arbustetum* or Thicket on the head of the Teazell, may be observed in this order. And he that considereth that fabrick so regularly palisadoed, and stemm'd with flowers of the royall colour; in the house of the solitary maggot, may finde the Seraglio of *Solomon*, And contemplating the calicular shafts, and uncous disposure of their extremities, so accommodable unto the office of abstersion, not condemne as wholly improbable the conceit of those who accept it for the herbe *Borith*. Where by the way, we could with much inquiry never discover any transfiguration, in this abstemious insect, although we have kept them long in their proper houses, and boxes. Where some wrapt up in their webbs, have lived upon their own bowels, from September unto July.

In such a grove doe walke the little creepers about the head of the burre. And such an order is observed in the aculeous prickly plantation, upon the heads of several common thistles, remarkably in the notable palisados about the flower of the milk-Thistle; and he that inquireth into the little bottome of the globe-thistle, may finde that gallant bush arise from a scalpe of like disposure.

The white umbrella or medicall bush of Elder, is an Epitome of this order: arising from five main stemms Quincuncially disposed, and tollerably maintained, in their subdivisions. To omit the lower observations in the seminal spike of Mercurie, weld, and Plantane.

Thus hath nature ranged the flowers of Santfoyne, and French honey suckle; and somewhat after this manner hath ordered the bush in *Jupiters* beard, or houseleek; which old superstitition set on the tops of houses, as a defensative against lightening, and thunder. The like in Fenny Sengreen or the water Souldier; which, though a militarie name from Greece, makes out the Roman order.

A like ordination there is in the favaginous Sockets, and Lozenge seeds of the noble flower of the Sunne. Wherein in Lozenge figured boxes nature shuts up the seeds, and balsame which is about them.

But the Firre and Pinetree from their fruits doe naturally dictate this position. The Rhomboidall protuberances in Pineapples maintaining this Quincuncial order unto each other, and each Rhombus in it selfe. Thus are also disposed the triangular foliations, in the conicall fruit of the firre tree, orderly shadowing and protecting the winged seeds below them.

The like so often occurreth to the curiosity of observers, especially in spicated seeds and flowers, that we shall not need to take in the single Quincunx of Fuchsius in the grouth of the masle fearn, the seedie disposure of Gramen Ischemon, and the trunk or neat Reticulate work in the codde of the Sachell palme.

For even in very many round stalk plants, the leaves are set after a Quintuple ordination, the first leaf answering the fifth, in lateral disposition. Wherein the leaves successively rounding the stalke, in foure at the furthest the compass is absolved, and the fifth leafe or sprout returns to the position of the other fifth before it; as in accounting upward is often observable in furze, pellitorye, Ragweed, the sproutes of Oaks, and thorns upon pollards, and very remarkably in the regular disposure of the rugged excrescencies in the yearly shoots of the Pine.

But in square stalked plants, the leaves stand respectively unto each other, either in crosse of decussation to those above or below them, arising at crosse positions; whereby they shadow not each other, and better resist the force of winds, which in a parallel situation, and upon square stalkes would more forcibly bear upon them.

And to omit, how leaves and sprouts which compasse not the stalk, are often set in a Rhomboides, and making long and short Diagonals, doe stand like the leggs of Quadrupeds when they goe: Nor to urge the thwart enclosure and furdling of flowers and blossomes before explication, as in the multi-plyed leaves of Pionie; And the Chiasmus in five leaved flowers, while one lies wrapt about the staminous beards, the other foure obliquely shutting and closing upon each other;

and how even flowers which consist of foure leaves stand not ordinarily in three and one, but two and two crossewise unto the Stylus; even the Autumnal budds, which awaite the returne of the sun, doe after the winter solstice multiply their calicular leaves, making little Rhombuses, and network figures, as in the Sycamore and Lilac.

The like is discoverable in the original production of plants, which first putting forth two leaves, those which succeed bear not over each other, but shoot obliquely or crossewise, untill the stalke appeareth; which sendeth not forth its first leaves without all order unto them; and he that from hence can discover in what position the two first leaves did arise, is no ordinary observator.

Where by the way, he that observeth the rudimental spring of seeds, shall finde strict rule, although not after this order. How little is required unto effectual generation, and in what diminutives the pastick principle lodgeth, is exemplified in seeds, wherein the greater mass affords so little comproduction. In Beanes the leaf and root sprout from the Germen, the main sides split, and lye by, and in some pull'd up near the time of blooming we have found the pulpous sides intire or little wasted. In Acorns the nebb dilating splitteth the two sides, which sometimes lye whole, when the Oak is sprouted two handfuls. In Lupins these pulpy sides do sometimes arise with the stalk in a resemblance of two fat leaves. Wheat and Rye will grow up, if after they have shot some tender Roots, the adhering pulp be taken from them. Beanes will prosper though a part be cut away, and so much set as sufficeth to contain and keep the Germen close. From this superfluous pulp, in unkindely and wet years, may arise that multiplicity of little insects, which infest the Roots and Sprouts of tender Graines and pulses.

In the little nebbe or fructifying principle, the motion is

regular, and not transvertible, as to make that ever the leaf, which nature intendeth the root; observable from their conversion, until they attain their right position, if seeds be set inversedly.

In vain we expect the production of plants from different parts of the seed, from the same *corculum* or little original proceed both germinations; and in the power of this slender particle lye many Roots and sproutings, that though the same be pull'd away, the generative particle will renew them again, and proceed to a perfect plant; And malt may be observed to grow, though the Cummes be fallen from it.

The seminall nebbe hath a defined and single place, and not extended unto both extremes. And therefore many too vulgarly conceive that Barley and Oats grow at both ends; For they arise from one *punctilio* or generative nebbe, and the Speare sliding under the husk, first appeareth nigh the toppe. But in Wheat and Rye being bare the sprouts are seen together. If Barley unhulled would grow, both would appear at once. But in this and Oat-meal the nebbe is broken away, which makes them the milder food, and lesse apt to raise fermentation in Decoctions.

Men taking notice of what is outwardly visible, conceive a sensible priority in the Root. But as they begin from one part, so they seem to start and set out upon one signall of nature. In Beans yet soft, in Pease while they adhere unto the Cod, the rudimentall Leafe and Root are discoverable. In the Seeds of Rocket and Mustard, sprouting in Glasses of water, when the one is manifest the other is also perceptible. In muddy waters apt to breed *Duckweed*, and Periwinkles, if the first and rudimentall stroaks of Duckweed be observed, the Leaves and Root anticipate not each other. But in the Date-stone the first sprout is neither root nor leaf distinctly, but both together; For the Germination being to passe through the narrow Navell and hole about the midst of the stone, the generative germ is faine to enlengthen it self, and shooting out about an inch, at that distance divideth into the ascending and descending portion.

And though it be generally thought that Seeds will root at that end, where they adhere to their Originals, and observable it is that the nebbe sets most often next the stalk, as in Grains, Pulses, and most small Seeds, yet is it hardly made out in many greater plants. For in Acornes, Almonds, Pistachios, Wallnuts, and accuminated shells, the germ puts forth at the remotest part of the pulp. And therefore to set Seeds in that posture, wherein the Leaf and Roots may shoot right without contortion, or forced circumvolution, which might render them strongly rooted, and straighter, were a Criticisme in Agriculture. And nature seems to have made some provision hereof in many from their figure, that as they fall from the tree they may lye in Positions agreeable to such advantages.

Beside the open and visible Testicles of plants, the seminall powers lie in great part invisible, while the Sun findes polypody in stone-wals, the little stinging Nettle and nightshade in barren sandy High-wayes, *Scurvy-grasse* in *Greeneland*, and unknown plants in earth brought from remote Countries. Beside the known longevity of some Trees, what is the most lasting herb, or seed, seems not easily determinable. Mandrakes upon known account have lived near an hundred yeares. Seeds found in Wilde-Fowls Gizards have sprouted in the earth. The Seeds of Marjorane and *Stramonium* carelessly kept, have grown after seven years. Even in Garden-plots long fallow, and digged up, the seeds of *Blattaria* and yellow henbane after twelve years burial have produced themselves again.

That bodies are first spirits *Paracelsus* could affirm, which in the maturation of Seeds and fruits, seems obscurely implied by *Aristotle*, when he delivereth, that the spirituous parts are converted into water, and the water into earth, and attested by observation in the maturative progresse of Seeds, wherein at first may be discerned a flatuous distension of the husk, afterwards a thin liquor, which longer time digesteth into a pulp or kernell observable in Almonds and large Nuts. And some way answered in the progressionall perfection of animall semination, in its spermaticall maturation, from crude pubescency unto perfection. And even that seeds themselves in their rudimentall discoveries, appear in foliaceous surcles, or sprouts within their coverings, in a diaphanous gellie, before deeper incrassation, is also visibly verified in Cherries, Acorns, Plums.

From seminall considerations, either in reference unto one another, or distinction from animall production, the holy Scripture describeth the vegetable creation; And while it divideth plants but into Herb and Tree, though it seemeth to make but an accidental division, from magnitude, it tacitely containeth the naturall distinction of vegetables, observed by Herbarists, and comprehending the four kinds. For since the most naturall distinction is made from the production of leaf or stalk, and plants after the two first seminall leaves do either proceed to send forth more leaves, or a stalk, and the folious and stalky emission distinguisheth herbs and trees, in a large acception it comprizeth all vegetables; for the *frutex* and *suffrutex* are under the progression of trees, and stand Authentically differenced but from the accidents of the stalk.

The Æquivocall production of things under undiscerned principles, makes a large part of generation, though they seem to hold a wide univocacy in their set and certain Originals, while almost every plant breeds its peculiar insect, most a Butterfly, moth or fly, wherein the Oak seems to contain the largest seminality, while the Julus, Oak-apple, pill, woolly tuft, foraminous roundles upon the leaf, and grapes under ground make a Fly with some difference. The great variety of Flyes lyes in the variety of their originals, in the seeds of Caterpillars or Cankers there lyeth not only a Butterfly or Moth, but if they be sterill or untimely cast, their production is often a Fly, which we have also observed from corrupted and mouldred Egges, both of Hens and Fishes; To omit the generation of Bees out of the bodies of dead Heifers, or what is strange yet well attested, the production of Eeles in the backs of living Cods and Perches.

The exiguity and smallnesse of some seeds extending to large productions is one of the magnalities of nature, somewhat illustrating the work of the Creation, and vast production from nothing. The true seeds of Cypresse and Rampions are indistinguishable by old eyes. Of the seeds of Tobacco a thousand make not one grain, The disputed seeds of Harts tongue, and Maidenhair, require a greater number. From such undiscernable seminalities arise spontaneous productions. He that would discern the rudimentall stroak of a plant, may behold it in the Originall of Duckweed, at the bignesse of a pins point, from convenient water in glasses, wherein a watchfull eye may also discover the puncticular Originals of Periwincles and Gnats.

That seeds of some Plants are lesse than any animals, seems of no clear decision; That the biggest of Vegetables exceedeth the biggest of Animals, in full bulk, and all dimensions, admits exception in the Whale, which in length and above ground measure, will also contend with tall Oakes. That the richest odour of plants surpasseth that of Animals may seem of some doubt, since animall-musk seems to excell the vegetable, and we find so noble a sent in the Tulip-Fly, and Goat-Beetle.

Now whether seminall nebbes hold any sure proportion

unto seminall enclosures, why the form of the germe doth not answer the figure of the enclosing pulp, why the nebbe is seated upon the solid, and not the channeld side of the seed as in grains, why since we often meet with two yolks in one shell, and sometimes one Egge within another, we do not oftener meet with two nebbes in one distinct seed: why since the Egges of a Hen laid at one course do commonly out-weigh the bird, and some moths coming out of their cases, without assistance of food, will lay so many Egges as to out-weigh their bodies, trees rarely bear their fruit in that gravity or proportion: Whether in the germination of seeds according to *Hippocrates*, the lighter part ascendeth, and maketh the sprout, the heaviest tending downward frameth the root; Since we observe that the first shoot of seeds in water will sink or bow down at the upper and leafing end: Whether it be not more rational Epicurisme to contrive whole dishes out of the nebbes and spirited particles of plants, than from the Gallatures and treddles of Egges; since that part is found to hold no seminal share in Oval Generation, are quæries which might enlarge but must conclude this digression.

And though not in this order, yet how nature delighteth in this number, and what consent and coordination there is in the leaves and parts of flowers, it cannot escape our observation in no small number of plants. For the calicular or supporting and closing leaves do answer the number of the flowers, especially in such as exceed not the number of Swallows Egges; as in Violets, Stichwort, Blossomes; and flowers of one leaf have often five divisions, answered by a like number of calicular leaves; as *Gentianella, Convolvulus*, Bell-flowers. In many the flowers, blades, or staminous shootes and leaves are all equally five, as in cockle, mullein and *Blattaria*; Wherein the flowers before explication are pentagonally wrappen up, with some resemblance of the *blatta* or moth from whence it hath its name: But the contrivance of nature is singular in the opening and shutting of Bindeweeds, performed by five inflexures, distinguishable by pyramidall figures, and also different colours.

The rose at first is thought to have been of five leaves, as it yet groweth wilde among us; but in the most luxuriant, the calicular leaves do still maintain that number. But nothing is more admired than the five Brethren of the Rose, and the strange disposure of the Appendices or Beards, in the calicular leaves thereof, which in despair of resolution is tolerably salved from this contrivance, best ordered and suited for the free closure of them before explication. For those two which are smooth, and of no beard, are contrived to lye undermost, as without prominent parts, and fit to be smoothly covered; the other two which are beset with Beards in either side, stand outward and uncovered, but the fifth or half-bearded leaf is covered on the bare side but on the open side stands free, and bearded like the other.

Besides a large number of leaves have five divisions, and may be circumscribed by a *Pentagon* or figure of five Angles, made by right lines from the extremity of their leaves, as in Maple, Vine, Figge-Tree: But five-leaved flowers are commonly disposed circularly about the *Stylus*; according to the higher Geometry of nature, dividing a circle by five *radii*, which concurre not to make Diameters, as in Quadrilaterall and sexangular Intersections.

Now the number of five is remarkable in every circle, not only as the first sphærical number, but the measure of sphærical motion. For sphærical bodies move by fives, and every globular figure placed upon a plane, in direct volutation, returns to the first point of contaction in the fifth touch, accounting by the Axes of the Diameters or Cardinall points of the four quarters thereof. And before it arriveth unto the same point again, it maketh five circles equall unto it self, in each progresse from those quarters absolving an equall circle.

By the same number doth nature divide the circle of the Sea-Starre, and in that order and number disposeth those elegant Semicircles, or dentall sockets and egges in the Sea Hedgehogge. And no mean Observations hereof there is in the Mathematicks of the neatest Retiary Spider, which concluding in fourty four Circles, from five Semidiameters beginneth that elegant texture.

And after this manner doth lay the foundation of the circular branches of the Oak, which being five-cornered, in the tender annual sprouts, and manifesting upon incision the signature of a Starre, is after made circular, and swel'd into a round body: Which practice of nature is become a point of art, and makes two Problemes in *Euclide*. But the Bramble which sends forth shoots and prickles from its angles, maintains its pentagonall figure, and the unobserved signature of a handsome porch within it. To omit the five small buttons dividing the Circle of the Ivy-berry, and the five characters in the Winter stalk of the Walnut, with many other Observables, which cannot escape the eyes of signal discerners; Such as know where to finde *Ajax* his name in *Delphinium*, or *Aarons* Mitre in Henbane.

Quincuncial forms and ordinations are also observable in animal figurations. For to omit the hioides of throat-bone of animals, the *furcula* or *merry-thought* in birds, which supporteth the *scapulæ*, affording a passage for the windepipe and the gullet, the wings of Flyes, and disposure of their legges in their first formation from maggots, and the position of their horns, wings and legges, in their *Aurelian* cases and swadling clouts: The back of the *Cimex Arboreus*, found often upon Trees and lesser plants, doth elegantly discover the *Burgundian* decussation; And the like is observable in the belly of the

Notonecton, or water-Beetle, which swimmeth on its back, and the handsome Rhombusses of the Sea-poult, or Weazell, on either side the Spine.

The sexangular Cels in the Honeycombs of Bees are disposed after this order. Much there is not of wonder in the confused Houses of Pismires, though much in their busie life and actions; more in the edificial Palaces of Bees and Monarchical spirits; who make their combs six-corner'd, declining a circle, whereof many stand not close together, and compleatly fill the *area* of the place; But rather affecting a six-sided figure, whereby every cell affords a common side unto six more, and also a fit receptacle for the Bee it self, which gathering into a Cylindrical Figure, aptly enters its sexangular house, more nearly approaching a circular Figure, than either doth the Square or Triangle. And the Combes themselves so regularly contrived, that their mutual intersections make three Lozenges at the bottome of every Cell; which severally regarded make three Rows of neat Rhomboidall Figures, connected at the angles, and so continue three several chains throughout the whole comb.

As for the *Favago* found commonly on the sea shoar, though named from an honey-comb, it but rudely makes out the resemblance, and better agrees with the round Cels of humble Bees. He that would exactly discern the shop of a Bees mouth, needs observing eyes, and good augmenting glasses; wherein is discoverable one of the neatest peeces in nature; and must have a more piercing eye than mine, who findes out the shape of Buls heads in the guts of Drones pressed out behinde, according to the experiment of *Gomesius*; wherein notwithstanding there seemeth somewhat which might incline a pliant fancy to credulity of similitude.

A resemblance hereof there is in the orderly and rarely disposed Cels, made by Flyes and Insects, which we have often found fastened about small sprigs, and in those cottonary and woolly pillows, which sometimes we meet with fastened unto Leaves, there is included an elegant Net-work Texture, out of which come many small Flies. And some resemblance there is of this order in the Egges of some Butterflies and moths, as they stick upon leaves, and other substances; which being dropped from behinde, nor directed by the eye, do neatly declare how nature Geometrizeth, and observeth order in all things.

A like correspondency in figure is found in the skins and outward teguments of animals, whereof a regardable part are beautiful by this texture. As the backs of several Snakes and Serpents, elegantly remarkable in the *Aspis*, and the Dart-snake, in the Chiasmus and larger decussations upon the back of the Rattlesnake, and in the close and finer texture of the *Mater formicarum*, or snake that delights in Anthils; whereby upon approach of outward injuries, they can raise a thicker Phalanx on their backs, and handsomely contrive themselves into all kindes of flexures: Whereas their bellies are commonly covered with smooth semicircular divisions, as best accommodable unto their quick and gliding motion.

This way is followed by nature in the peculiar and remarkable tayl of the Bever, wherein the scaly particles are disposed somewhat after this order, which is the plainest resolution of the wonder of *Bellonius*, while he saith, with incredible Artifice hath Nature framed the tayl or Oar of the Bever: where by the way we cannot but wish a model of their houses, so much extolled by some Describers: wherein since they are so bold as to venture upon three stages, we might examine their Artifice in the contignations, the rule and order in the compartitions; or whether that magnified structure be any more than a rude rectangular pyle or meer hovell-building.

Thus works the hand of nature in the feathery plantation

about birds. Observable in the skins of the breast, legs and Pinions of Turkies, Geese, and Ducks, and the Oars or finny feet of Water-Fowl: And such a naturall Net is the scaly covering of Fishes, of Mullets, Carps, Tenches, &c. even in such as are excoriable and consist of smaller scales, as Bretts, Soals, and Flounders. The like Reticulate grain is observable in some *Russia* Leather. To omit the ruder Figures of the ostracion, the triangular or cunny fish, or the pricks of the Sea-Porcupine.

The same is also observable in some part of the skin of man, in habits of neat texture, and therefore not unaptly compared unto a Net: We shall not affirm that from such grounds the Ægyptian Embalmers imitated this texture, yet in their linnen folds the same is still observable among their neatest Mummies, in the figures of *Isis* and *Osyris*, and the Tutelary spirits in the Bembine Table. Nor is it to be overlooked how *Orus*, the Hieroglyphick of the world, is described in a Net-work covering, from the shoulder to the foot. And (not to enlarge upon the cruciated character of *Trismegistus*, or handed crosses, so often occurring in the Needles of *Pharaoh*, and Obelisks of Antiquity) the *Statuæ Isiacæ*, Teraphims, and little Idols, found about the Mummies, do make a decussation or *Jacobs* Crosse with their armes, like that on the head of *Ephraim* and *Manasses*, and this *decussis* is also graphically described between them.

This Reticulate or Net-work was also considerable in the inward parts of man, not only from the first *subtegmen* or warp of his formation, but in the netty *fibres* of the veins and vessels of life; wherein according to common Anatomy the right and transverse *fibres* are decussated by the oblique *fibres*; and so must frame a Reticulate and Quincunciall Figure by their Obliquations, Emphatically extending that Elegant expression of Scripture: Thou hast curiously embroydered me, thou hast wrought me up after the finest way of texture, and as it were with a Needle.

Nor is the same observable only in some parts, but in the whole body of man, which upon the extension of arms and legges, doth make out a square, whose intersection is at the genitals. To omit the phantastical Quincunx, in *Plato*, of the first Hermaphrodite or double man, united at the Loynes, which *Jupiter* after divided.

A rudimentall resemblance hereof there is in the cruciated and rugged folds of the *Reticulum*, or Net-like Ventricle of ruminating horned animals, which is the second in order, and culinarily called the Honey-comb. For many divisions there are in the stomack of severall animals; what number they maintain in the *Scarus* and ruminating Fish, common description or our own experiment hath made no discovery. But in the Ventricle of *Porpuses* there are three divisions. In many Birds a crop, Gizard, and little receptacle before it; but in Cornigerous animals, which chew the cudd, there are no less than four of distinct position and office.

The *Reticulum* by these crossed cels makes a further digestion, in the dry and exuccous part of the Aliment received from the first Ventricle. For at the bottome of the gullet there is a double Orifice; What is first received at the mouth descendeth into the first and greater stomack, from whence it is returned into the mouth again; and after a fuller mastication, and salivous mixture, what part thereof descendeth again, in a moist and succulent body, it slides down the softer and more permeable Orifice, into the Omasus or third stomack; and from thence conveyed into the fourth, receives its last digestion. The other dry and exuccous part after rumination by the larger and stronger orifice beareth into the first stomack, from thence into the *Reticulum*, and so progressively into the other divisions. And therefore in

Calves newly calved, there is little or no use of the two first Ventricles, for the milk and liquid aliment slippeth down the softer Orifice, into the third stomack; where making little or no stay, it passeth into the fourth, the seat of the *Coagulum*, or Runnet, or that division of stomack which seems to bear the name of the whole, in the Greek translation of the Priests Fee, in the Sacrifice of Peace-offerings.

As for those Rhomboidal Figures made by the Cartilagineous parts of the Wezon, in the Lungs of great Fishes, and other animals, as *Rondeletius* discovered, we have not found them so to answer our figure as to be drawn into illustration; Something we expected in the more discernable texture of the lungs of frogs, which notwithstanding being but two curious bladders not weighing above a grain, we found interwoven with veins not observing any just order. More orderly situated are those cretaceous and chalky concretions found sometimes in the bignesse of a small fech on either side their spine; which being not agreeable unto our order, nor yet observed by any, we shall not here discourse on.

But had we found a better account and tolerable Anatomy of that prominent jowle of the *Sperma Ceti* Whale, than questuary operation, or the stench of the last cast upon our shoar, permitted, we might have perhaps discovered some handsome order in those Net-like creases and sockets, made like honey-combs, containing that medicall matter.

Lastly, The incession of locall motion of animals is made with analogy unto this figure, by decussative diametrals, Quincunciall Lines and angles. For to omit the enquiry how Butterflies and breezes move their four wings, how birds and fishes in ayre and water move by joynt stroaks of opposite wings and Finnes, and how salient animals in jumping forward seem to arise and fall upon a square base; As the station of most Quadrupeds is made upon a long square, so in their motion they make a Rhomboides; their common progression being performed Diametrally, by decussation and crosse advancement of their legges, which not observed begot that remarkable absurdity in the position of the legges of *Castors* horse in the Capitol. The Snake which moveth circularly makes his spires in like order, the convex and concave spirals answering each other at alternate distances; In the motion of man the armes and legges observe this thwarting position, but the legges alone do move Quincuncially by single angles with some resemblance of a V measured by successive advancement from each foot, and the angle of indenture great or lesse, according to the extent or brevity of the stride.

Studious Observators may discover more analogies in the orderly book of nature, and cannot escape the Elegancy of her hand in other correspondencies. The Figures of nails and crucifying appurtenances, are but precariously made out in the *Granadilla* or flower of Christs passion: And we despair to behold in these parts that handsome draught of crucifixion in the fruit of the *Barbado* Pine. The seminal Spike of *Phalaris*, or great shaking grasse, more nearly answers the tayl of a Rattle-Snake than many resemblances in *Porta*: And if the man *Orchis* of *Columna* be well made out, it excelleth all analogies. In young Wallnuts cut athwart, it is not hard to apprehend strange characters; and in those of somewhat elder growth, handsome ornamental draughts about a plain crosse. In the root of *Osmond* or Water fern, every eye may discern the form of a Half Moon, Rain-bow, or half the character of Pisces. Some finde Hebrew, Arabick, Greek, and Latine Characters in Plants; In a common one among us we seem to reade *Aiaia, Viviu, Lilil.*

Right lines and circles make out the bulk of plants; In the parts thereof we finde Helicall or spirall roundles, voluta's,

conicall Sections, circular Pyramids, and frustums of *Archi-*
medes; And cannot overlook the orderly hand of nature, in
the alternate succession of the flat and narrower sides in the
tender shoots of the Ashe, or the regular inequality of bignesse
in the five-leaved flowers of Henbane, and something like in
the calicular leaves of *Tutson*. How the spots of *Persicaria*
do manifest themselves between the sixt and tenth ribbe. How
the triangular capp in the stemme or *stylus* of Tuleps doth
constantly point at three outward leaves. That spicated
flowers do open first at the stalk. That white flowers have
yellow thrums or knops. That the nebbe of Beans and Pease
do all look downward, and so presse not upon each other;
And how the seeds of many pappous or downy flowers lockt
up in sockets, after a gomphosis or *mortis*-articulation, diffuse
themselves circularly into branches of rare order, observable
in *Tragopogon* or Goats-beard, conformable to the Spiders
web, and the *Radii* in like manner telarely inter-woven.

And how in animall natures, even colours hold correspondencies, and mutuall correlations. That the colour of the
Caterpillar will shew again in the Butterfly, with some latitude
is allowable. Though the regular spots in their wings seem
but a mealie adhesion, and such as may be wiped away, yet
since they come in this variety out of their cases, there must
be regular pores in those parts and membranes, defining such
Exudations.

That *Augustus* had native notes on his body and belly,
after the order and number in the Starres of *Charles wayne*,
will not seem strange unto astral Physiognomy, which accordingly considereth moles in the body of man, or Physicall
Observators, who from the position of moles in the face,
reduce them to rule and correspondency in other parts.
Whether after the like method medicall conjecture may not
be raised, upon parts inwardly affected; since parts about the

lips are the critical seats of Pustules discharged in Agues; And scrophulous tumours about the neck do so often speak the like about the Mesentery, may also be considered.

The russet neck in young Lambs seems but adventitious, and may owe its tincture to some contaction in the womb; But that if sheep have any black or deep russet in their faces, they want not the same about their legges and feet; That black Hounds have mealy mouths and feet; That black Cows which have any white in their tayls, should not misse of some in their bellies; and if all white in their bodies, yet if black-mouth'd, their ears and feet maintain the same colour, are correspondent tinctures not ordinarily failing in nature, which easily unites the accidents of extremities, since in some generations she transmutes the parts themselves, while in the *Aurelian Metamorphosis* the head of the canker becomes the Tayl of the Butterfly. Which is in some way not beyond the contrivance of Art, in submersions and Inlays, inverting the extremes of the plant, and fetching the root from the top, and also imitated in handsome columnary work, in the inversion of the extremes; wherein the Capitel, and the Base, hold such near correspondency.

In the motive parts of animals may be discovered mutuall proportions; not only in those of Quadrupeds, but in the thigh-bone, legge, foot-bone, and claws of Birds. The legs of Spiders are made after a sesqui-tertian proportion, and the long legs of some locusts, double unto some others. But the internodial parts of Vegetables, or spaces between the joints are contrived with more uncertainty; though the joints themselves in many plants maintain a regular number.

In vegetable composure, the unition of prominent parts seems most to answer the *Apophyses* or processes of Animall bones, whereof they are the produced parts or prominent explantations. And though in the parts of plants which are not ordained for motion, we do not expect correspondent Articulations; yet in the setting on of some flowers, and seeds in their sockets, and the lineal commissure of the pulpe of severall seeds, may be observed some shadow of the Harmony; some show of the Gomphosis or *mortis*-articulation.

As for the Diarthrosis or motive Articulation, there is expected little Analogy, though long-stalked leaves doe move by long lines, and have observable motions, yet are they made by outward impulsion, like the motion of pendulous bodies, while the parts themselves are united by some kinde of *symphysis* unto the stock.

But standing vegetables, void of motive-Articulations, are not without many motions. For beside the motion of vegetation upward, and of radiation unto all quarters, that of contraction, dilatation, inclination, and contortion, is discoverable in many plants. To omit the rose of *Jericho*, the ear of Rye, which moves with change of weather, and the Magical spit, made of no rare plants, which windes before the fire, and rosts the bird without turning.

Even Animals near the Classis of plants, seem to have the most restlesse motions. The Summer-worm of Ponds and plashes makes a long waving motion; the hair-worm seldome lies still. He that would behold a very anomalous motion, may observe it in the Tortile and tiring stroakes of Gnatworms.

CHAPTER IV

As for the delights, commodities, mysteries, with other concernments of this order, we are unwilling to fly them over, in the short deliveries of *Virgil*, *Varro*, or others, and shall therefore enlarge with additionall ampliations.

By this position they had a just proportion of Earth, to supply an equality of nourishment. The distance being ordered, thick or thin, according to the magnitude or vigorous attraction of the plant, the goodnesse, leannesse, or propriety of the soyle; and therefore the rule of *Solon*, concerning the territory of *Athens*, not extendible unto all; allowing the distance of six foot unto common Trees, and nine for the Figge and Olive.

They had a due diffusion of their roots on all or both sides, whereby they maintained some proportion to their height, in Trees of large radication. For that they strictly make good their profundeur or depth unto their height, according to common conceit, and that expression of *Virgil*, though confirmable from the plane Tree in *Pliny*, and some few examples, is not to be expected from the generallitie of Trees almost in any kinde, either of side-spreading, or tap-roots: Except we measure them by lateral and opposite diffusions; nor commonly to be found in *minor* or hearby plants; If we except Sea-holly, Liquorish, Sea-rush, and some others.

They had a commodious radiation in their growth; and a due expansion of their branches, for shadow or delight. For trees thickly planted do runne up in height and branch with no expansion, shooting unequally or short, and thinne upon the neighbouring side. And therefore Trees are inwardly bare, and spring and leaf from the outward and Sunny side of their branches.

Whereby they also avoided the perill of συνολεθρία or one

tree perishing with another, as it happeneth ofttimes from the sick *effluviums* or entanglements of the roots, falling foul with each other. Observable in Elmes set in hedges, where if one dieth the neighbouring Tree prospereth not long after.

In this situation divided into many intervals and open unto six passages, they had the advantage of a fair perflation from windes, brushing and cleansing their surfaces, relaxing and closing their pores unto due perspiration. For that they afford large e*ffluviums* perceptible from odours, diffused at great distances, is observable from Onyons out of the earth; which though dry, and kept until the spring, as they shoot forth large and many leaves, do notably abate of their weight. And mint growing in glasses of water, until it arriveth unto the weight of an ounce, in a shady place, will sometimes exhaust a pound of water.

And as they send forth much, so may they receive somewhat in: For beside the common way road and of reception by the root, there may be a refection and imbibition from without; For gentle showrs refresh plants, though they enter not their roots; And the good and bad *effluviums* of Vegetables promote or debilitate each other. So *Epithymum* and *Dodder*, rootlesse and out of the ground, maintain themselves upon Thyme, Savory, and plants, whereon they hang. And *Ivy* divided from the root, we have observed to live some years, by the cirrous parts commonly conceived but as tenacles and holdfasts unto it. The stalks of mint cropt from the root stripped from the leaves, and set in *glasses* with the root end upward & out of the water, we have observed to send forth sprouts and leaves without the aid of roots, and *scordium* to grow in like manner, the leaves set downward in water. To omit several Sea-plants, which grow on single roots from stones, although in very many there are side-shoots and *fibres*, beside the fastening root.

By this open position they were fairly exposed unto the rayes of Moon and Sunne, so considerable in the growth of Vegetables. For though Poplars, Willows, and several Trees be made to grow about the brinks of *Acharon*, and dark habitations of the dead; Though some plants are content to grow in obscure Wells; wherein also old Elme pumps afford sometimes long bushy sprouts, not observable in any aboveground: And large fields of Vegetables are able to maintain their verdure at the bottome and shady part of the Sea; yet the greatest number are not content without the actual rayes of the Sunne, but bend, incline, and follow them; As large lists of solisequious and Sun-following plants. And some observe the method of its motion in their owne growth and conversion, twining towards the West by the South, as Bryony, Hops, Woodbine, and several kindes of Bindeweed; which we shall more admire, when any can tell us, they observe another motion, and Twist by the North at the *Antipodes*. The same plants rooted against an erect North-wall full of holes, will finde a way through them to look upon the Sunne. And in tender plants from mustard seed, sown in the winter, and in a pot of earth placed inwardly in a chamber against a South-window, the tender stalks of two leaves arose not erect, but bending towards the window, nor looking much higher than the Meridian Sun. And if the pot were turned they would work themselves into their former declinations, making their conversion by the East. That the Leaves of the Olive and some other Trees solstitially turn, and precisely tell us, when the Sun is entred *Cancer*, is scarce expectable in any Climate; and *Theophrastus* warily observes it; Yet somewhat thereof is observable in our own, in the leaves of Willows and Sallows, some weeks after the Solstice. But the great *Convolvulus* or white-flower'd *Bindweed* observes both motions of the Sunne: while the flower twists Æquinoctionally from the left hand to the right, according to the daily revolution, The stalk twineth ecliptically from the right to the left, according to the annual conversion.

Some commend the exposure of these orders unto the Western gales, as the most generative and fructifying breath of heaven. But we applaud the Husbandry of *Solomon*, whereto agreeth the doctrine of *Theophrastus*: Arise O North-winde, and blow thou South upon my garden, that the spices thereof may flow out; for the North-winde closing the pores, and shutting up the *effluviums*, when the South doth after open and relax them, the Aromatical gummes do drop, and sweet odours fly actively from them. And if his garden had the same situation, which mapps and charts afford it, on the East side of *Jerusalem*, and having the wall on the West; these were the windes unto which it was well exposed.

By this way of plantation they encreased the number of their trees, which they lost in *Quaternio's*, and square-orders, which is a commodity insisted on by *Varro*, and one great intent of nature, in this position of flowers and seeds in the elegant formation of plants, and the former Rules observed in naturall and artificiall Figurations.

Whether in this order and one Tree in some measure breaking the cold and pinching gusts of windes from the other, trees will not better maintain their inward circles, and either escape or moderate their excentricities, may also be considered. For the circles in Trees are naturally concentricall, parallell unto the bark, and unto each other, till frost and piercing windes contract and close them on the weather-side, the opposite semicircle widely enlarging, and at a comely distance, which hindreth ofttimes the beauty and roundnesse of Trees and makes the Timber lesse serviceable; whiles the ascending juyce not readily passing, settles in knots and inequalities. And therefore it is no new course of Agriculture, to observe the native position of Trees according to North and South in their transplantations.

The same is also observable underground in the circinations and sphærical rounds of Onyons, wherein the circles of the Orbes are ofttimes larger, and the meridionall lines stand wider upon one side than the other. And where the largenesse will make up the number of planetical Orbes, that of *Luna* and the lower planets excede the dimensions of *Saturne* and the higher: Whether the like be not verified in the Circles of the large roots of Briony and Mandrakes, or why in the knotts of Deale or Firre the Circles are often eccentricall, although not in a plane, but vertical and right position, deserves a further enquiry.

Whether there be not some irregularity of roundnesse in most plants according to their position? Whether some small compression of pores be not perceptible in parts which stand against the current of waters, as in Reeds, Bullrushes, and other vegetables toward the streaming quarter, may also be observed; and therefore such as are long and weak are commonly contrived into a roundnesse of figure, whereby the water presseth lesse, and slippeth more smoothly from them, and even in flags of flat-figured leaves, the greater part obvert their sharper sides unto the current in ditches.

But whether plants which float upon the surface of the water be for the most part of cooling qualities, those which shoot above it of heating vertues, and why? whether *Sargasso* for many miles floating upon the Western Ocean, or Sealettuce, and Phasganium at the bottome of our Seas, make good the like qualities? Why Fenny waters afford the hottest and sweetest plants, as Calamus, Cyperus, and Crowfoot, and mudd cast out of ditches most naturally produceth Arsmart? Why plants so greedy of water so little regard oyl? Why since many seeds contain much oyle within them, they

endure it not well without, either in their growth or production?
Why since Seeds shoot commonly under ground, and out of
the ayre, those which are let fall in shallow glasses, upon the
surface of the water, will sooner sprout than those at the
bottome? And if the water be covered with oyle, those at the
bottome will hardly sprout at all, we have not room to conjecture.

Whether Ivy would not lesse offend the Trees in this clean
ordination, and well kept paths, might perhaps deserve the
question. But this were a quæry only unto some habitations,
and little concerning *Cyrus* or the Babylonian territory;
wherein by no industry *Harpalus* could make Ivy grow: And
Alexander hardly found it about those parts to imitate the
pomp of *Bacchus*. And though in these Northern Regions
we are too much acquainted with one Ivy, we know too little
of another, whereby we apprehend not the expressions of
Antiquity, the Splenetick medicine of *Galen*, and the Emphasis
of the Poet, in the beauty of the white Ivy.

The like concerning the growth of Misseltoe, which depen-
deth not only of the *species*, or kinde of Tree, but much also
of the Soil. And therefore common in some places, not readily
found in others, frequent in *France*, not so common in *Spain*,
and scarce at all in the Territory of *Ferrara*: Nor easily to be
found where it is most required upon Oaks, lesse on Trees
continually verdant. Although in some places the Olive
escapeth it not, requiting its detriment in the delightfull view
of its red Berries; as *Clusius* observed in *Spain*, and *Bellonius*
about *Hierusalem*. But this Parasiticall plant suffers nothing
to grow upon it, by any way of art; nor could we ever make
it grow where nature had not planted it; as we have in vain
attempted by inocculation and incision, upon its native or
forreign stock. And though there seem nothing improbable
in the seed, it hath not succeeded by sation in any manner of

ground, wherein we had no reason to despair, since we reade of vegetable horns, and how Rams horns will root about *Goa*.

But besides these rurall commodities, it cannot be meanly delectable in the variety of Figures, which these orders, open and closed, do make. Whilest every inclosure makes a *Rhombus*, the figures obliquely taken a Rhomboides, the intervals bounded with parallell lines, and each intersection built upon a square, affording two Triangles or Pyramids vertically conjoyned; which in the strict Quincunciall order doe oppositely make acute and blunt Angles.

And though therein we meet not with right angles, yet every Rhombus containing four Angles equall unto four right, it virtually contains four right. Nor is this strange unto such as observe the naturall lines of Trees, and parts disposed in them. For neither in the root doth nature affect this angle, which shooting downward for the stability of the plant, doth best effect the same by Figures of Inclination; Nor in the Branches and stalky leaves, which grow most at acute angles; as declining from their head the root, and diminishing their Angles with their altitude: Verified also in lesser Plants, whereby they better support themselves, and bear not so heavily upon the stalk: So that while near the root they often make an Angle of seventy parts, the sprouts near the top will often come short of thirty. Even in the nerves and master veins of the leaves the acute angle ruleth; the obtuse but seldome found, and in the backward part of the leaf, reflecting and arching about the stalk. But why ofttimes one side of the leaf is unequall unto the other, as in Hazell and Oaks, why on either side the master vein the lesser and derivative channels stand not directly opposite, nor at equall angles, respectively unto the adverse side, but those of one part do often exceed the other, as the Wallnut and many more, deserves another enquiry.

Now if for this order we affect coniferous and tapering trees, particularly the Cypresse, which grows in a conicall figure; we have found a Tree not only of great Ornament, but in its Essentials of affinity unto this order. A solid Rhombus being made by the conversion of two Equicrurall Cones, as *Archimedes* hath defined. And these were the common Trees about *Babylon*, and the East, whereof the Ark was made; and *Alexander* found no Trees so accomodable to build his Navy; And this we rather think to be the Tree mentioned in the Canticles, which stricter Botanology will hardly allow to be Camphire.

And if delight or ornamentall view invite a comely disposure by circular amputations, as is elegantly performed in Hawthorns; then will they answer the figures made by the conversion of a Rhombus, which maketh two concentricall Circles; the greater circumference being made by the lesser angles, the lesser by the greater.

The Cylindrical figure of Trees is virtually contained and latent in this order. A Cylinder or long round being made by the conversion or turning of a Parallelogram, and most handsomely by a long square, which makes an equall, strong, and lasting figure in Trees, agreeable unto the body and motive parts of animals, the greatest number of Plants, and almost all roots, though their stalks be angular, and of many corners, which seem not to follow the figure of their Seeds; Since many angular Seeds send forth round stalks, and sphæricall seeds arise from angular spindles, and many rather conform unto their Roots, as the round stalks of bulbous Roots, and in tuberous Roots stemmes of like figure. But why since the largest number of Plants maintain a circular Figure, there are so few with teretous or long round leaves; why coniferous Trees are tenuifolious or narrow-leafed, why Plants of few or no joynts have commonly round stalks, why the greatest number of hollow stalks are round stalks; or why in this variety of angular stalks the quadrangular most exceedeth, were too long a speculation; Mean while obvious experience may finde, that in Plants of divided leaves above, nature often beginneth circularly in the two first leaves below, while in the singular plant of Ivy she exerciseth a contrary Geometry, and beginning with angular leaves below, rounds them in the upper branches.

Nor can the rows in this order want delight, as carrying an aspect answerable unto the *dipteros hypœthros*, or double order of columns open above; the opposite ranks of Trees standing like pillars in the *Cavedia* of the Courts of famous buildings, and the *Portico's* of the *Templa subdialia* of old; Somewhat imitating the *Peristylia* or Cloyster buildings, and the *Exedræ* of the Ancients, wherein men discoursed, walked and exercised; For that they derived the rule of Columnes from Trees, especially in their proportionall diminutions, is illustrated by *Vitruvius* from the shafts of Firre and Pine. And though the inter-arborations do imitate the *Areostylos*, or thin order, not strictly answering the proportion of intercolumniations; yet in many Trees they will not exceed the intermission of the Columnes in the Court of the Tabernacle; which being an hundred cubits long, and made up by twenty pillars, will afford no less than intervals of five cubits.

Beside, in this kinde of aspect the sight being not diffused but circumscribed between long parallels and the ἐπισκιασμὸς and adumbration from the branches, it frameth a penthouse over the eye, and maketh a quiet vision: And therefore in diffused and open aspects, men hollow their hand above their eye, and make an artificiall brow, whereby they direct the dispersed rayes of sight, and by this shade preserve a moderate light in the chamber of the eye; keeping the *pupilla* plump and fair, and not contracted or shrunk as in light and vagrant vision.

And therefore providence hath arched and paved the great house of the world, with colours of mediocrity, that is, blew and green, above and below the sight, moderately terminating the *acies* of the eye. For most plants, though green above-ground, maintain their Originall white below it, according to the candour of their seminall pulp, and the rudimental leaves do first appear in that colour; observable in Seeds sprouting in water upon their first foliation. Green seeming to be the first supervenient, or above-ground complexion of Vegetables, separable in many upon ligature or inhumation, as Succory, Endive, Artichoaks, and which is also lost upon fading in the Autumn.

And this is also agreeable unto water it self, the alimental vehicle or plants, which first altereth into this colour; And containing many vegetable seminalities, revealeth their Seeds by greennesse; and therefore soonest expected in rain or standing water, not easily found in distilled or water strongly boiled; wherein the Seeds are extinguished by fire and decoction, and therefore last long and pure without such alteration, affording neither uliginous coats, gnatworms, Acari, hair-worms, like crude and common water; And therefore most fit for wholsome beverage, and with malt makes Ale and Beer without boyling. What large water-drinkers some Plants are, the Canary-Tree and Birches in some Northern Countries, drenching the Fields about them do sufficiently demonstrate. How water it self is able to maintain the growth of Vegetables, and without extinction of their generative or medicall vertues; Beside the experiment of *Helmonts* tree, we have found in some which have lived six years in glasses. The seeds of Scurvy-grasse growing in waterpots have been fruitfull in the Land; and *Asarum* after a years space, and once casting its leaves in water, in the second leaves hath handsomely performed its vomiting operation.

Nor are only dark and green colors, but shades and shadows contrived through the great Volume of nature, and trees ordained not only to protect and shadow others, but by their shades and shadowing parts, to preserve and cherish themselves. The whole radiation or branchings shadowing the stock and the root, the leaves, the branches and fruit, too much exposed to the windes and scorching Sunne. The calicular leaves inclose the tender flowers, and the flowers themselves lye wrapt about the seeds, in their rudiment and first formations, which being advanced the flowers fall away; and are therefore contrived in variety of figures, best satisfying the intention; Handsomely observable in hooded and gaping flowers, and the Butterfly bloomes of leguminous plants, the lower leaf closely involving the rudimental Cod, and the alary or wingy divisions embracing or hanging over it.

But Seeds themselves do lie in perpetual shades, either under the leaf, or shut up in coverings; And such as lye barest, have their husks, skins, and pulps about them, wherein the nebbe and generative particle lyeth moist and secured from the injury of Ayre and Sunne. Darknesse and light hold inter-changeable dominions, and alternately rule the seminal state of things. Light unto *Pluto* is darknesse unto *Jupiter*. Legions of seminall *Idæa's* lye in their second Chaos and *Orcus* of *Hipocrates*; till putting on the habits of their forms, they shew themselves upon the stage of the world, and open dominion of *Jove*. They that held the Stars of heaven were but rayes and flashing glimpses of the Empyreall light, through holes and perforations of the upper heaven, took of the natural shadows of stars, while according to better discovery the poor Inhabitants of the Moone have but a polary life, and must passe half their dayes in the shadow of that Luminary.

Light that makes things seen, makes some things invisible: were it not for darknesse and the shadow of the earth, the noblest part of the Creation had remained unseen, and the Stars in heaven as invisible as on the fourth day, when they were created above the Horizon, with the Sun, or there was not an eye to behold them. The greatest mystery of Religion is expressed by adumbration, and in the noblest part of Jewish Types, we finde the Cherubims shadowing the Mercy-seat: Life it self is but the shadow of death, and souls departed but the shadows of the living: All things fall under this name. The Sunne it self is but the dark *simulachrum*, and light but the shadow of God.

Lastly, It is no wonder that this Quincunciall order was first and still affected as gratefull unto the Eye: For all things are seen Quincuncially; For at the eye the Pyramidal rayes from the object, receive a decussation, and so strike a second base upon the *Retina* or hinder coat, the proper organ of Vision; wherein the pictures from objects are represented, answerable to the paper, or wall in the dark chamber; after the decussation of the rayes at the hole of the hornycoat, and their refraction upon the Christalline humour, answering the *foramen* of the window, and the *convex* or burning-glasses, which refract the rayes that enter it. And if ancient Anatomy would hold, a like disposure there was of the optick or visual nerves in the brain, wherein Antiquity conceived a concurrence by decussation. And this not only observable in the Laws of direct Vision, but in some part also verified in the reflected rayes of sight. For making the angle of incidence equal to that of reflexion, the visual raye returneth Quincuncially, and after the form of a V, and the line of reflexion being continued unto the place of vision, there ariseth a semi-decussation, which makes the object seen in a perpendicular unto it self, and as farre below the reflectent, as it is from it above; observable in the Sun and Moon beheld in water.

And this is also the law of reflexion in moved bodies and

sounds, which though not made by decussation, observe the rule of equality between incidence and reflexion; whereby whispering places are framed by Ellipticall arches laid side-wise; where the voice being delivered at the *focus* of one extremity, observing an equality unto the angle of incidence, it will reflect unto the *focus* of the other end, and so escape the ears of the standers in the middle.

A like rule is observed in the reflection of the vocall and sonorous line in Ecchoes, which cannot therefore be heard in all stations. But happening in woody plantations, by waters, and able to return some words, if reacht by a pleasant and well-dividing voice, there may be heard the softest notes in nature.

And this not only verified in the way of sence, but in animall and intellectuall receptions. Things entring upon the intellect by a Pyramid from without, and thence into the memory by another from within, the common decussation being in the understanding as is delivered by *Bovillus*. Whether the intellectual and phantastical lines be not thus rightly disposed, but magnified, diminished, distorted, and ill placed in the Mathematicks of some brains, whereby they have irregular apprehensions of things, perverted notions, conceptions, and incurable hallucinations, were no unpleasant speculation.

And if Ægyptian Philosophy may obtain, the scale of influences was thus disposed, and the geniall spirits of both worlds do trace their way in ascending and descending Pyramids, mystically apprehended in the Letter X, and the open Bill and stradling Legges of a Stork, which was imitated by that Character.

Of this Figure *Plato* made choice to illustrate the motion of the soul, both of the world and man; while he delivereth that God divided the whole conjunction length-wise, according to the figure of a Greek χ, and then turning it about reflected it into a circle; By the circle implying the uniform motion of the first Orb, and by the right lines, the planetical and various motions within it. And this also with application unto the soul of man, which hath a double aspect, one right, whereby it beholdeth the body, and objects without; another circular and reciprocal, whereby it beholdeth it self. The circle declaring the motion of the indivisible soul, simple, according to the divinity of its nature, and returning into it self; the right lines respecting the motion pertaining unto sense, and vegetation, and the central decussation, the wondrous connexion of the severall faculties conjointly in one substance. And so conjoyned the unity and duality of the soul, and made out the three substances so much considered by him; That is, the indivisible or divine, the divisible or corporeal, and that third, which was the *Systasis* or harmony of those two, in the mystical decussation.

And if that were clearly made out which *Justin Martyr* took for granted, this figure hath had the honour to characterize and notifie our blessed Saviour, as he delivereth in that borrowed expression from *Plato*; *Decussavit eum in universo*, the hint whereof he would have *Plato* derive from the figure of the brazen Serpent, and to have mistaken the Letter X for T, whereas it is not improbable, he learned these and other mystical expressions in his Learned Observations of Ægypt, where he might obviously behold the Mercurial characters, the handed crosses, and other mysteries not thoroughly understood in the sacred Letter X, which being derivative from the Stork, one of the ten sacred animals, might be originally Ægyptian, and brought into *Greece* by *Cadmus* of that Countrey.

CHAPTER V

To enlarge this contemplation unto all the mysteries and secrets, accomodable unto this number, were inexcusable Pythagorisme, yet cannot omit the ancient conceit of five surnamed the number of justice; as justly dividing between the digits, and hanging in the centre of Nine, described by square numeration, which angularly divided will make the decussated number; and so agreeable unto the Quincunciall Ordination, and rowes divided by Equality, and just *decorum*, in the whole com-plantation; And might be the Originall of that common game among us, wherein the fifth place is Soveraigne, and carrieth the chief intention. The Ancients wisely instructing youth, even in their recreations unto virtue, that is, early to drive at the middle point and Central Seat of justice.

Nor can we omit how agreeable unto this number an handsome division is made in Trees and Plants, since *Plutarch* and the Ancients have named it the Divisive Number, justly dividing the Entities of the world, many remarkable things in it, and also comprehending the generall division of Vegetables. And he that considers how most blossomes of Trees, and greatest number of Flowers, consist of five leaves; and therein doth rest the setled rule of nature; So that in those which exceed there is often found, or easily made a variety; may readily discover how nature rests in this number, which is indeed the first rest and pause of numeration in the fingers, the naturall Organs thereof. Nor in the division of the feet of perfect animals doth nature exceed this account. And even in the joints of feet, which in birds are most multiplied, surpasseth not this number; So progressionally making them out in many, that from five in the fore-claw she descendeth unto two in the hindemost; And so in fower feet makes up the number of joynts, in the five fingers or toes of man.

Not to omit the Quintuple Section of a Cone, of handsome practise in Ornamentall Garden-plots, and in some way discoverable in so many works of Nature; In the leaves, fruits, and seeds of Vegetables, and scales of some Fishes, so much considerable in glasses, and the optick doctrine; wherein the learned may consider the Crystalline humour of the eye in the cuttle fish and *Loligo*.

He that forgets not how Antiquity named this the Conjugall or wedding number, and made it the Embleme of the most remarkable conjunction, will conceive it duely appliable unto this handsome Oeconomy, and vegetable combination; May hence apprehend the allegoricall sense of the obscure expression of *Hesiod*, and afford no improbable reason why *Plato* admitted his Nuptiall guests by fives, in the kindred of the married couple.

And though a sharper mystery might be implied in the Number of the five wise and foolish Virgins, which were to meet the Bridegroom, yet was the same agreeable unto the Conjugall Number, which ancient Numerists made out by two and three, the first parity and imparity, the active and passive digits, the materiall and formall principles in generative Societies. And not discordant even from the customes of the *Romans*, who admitted but five Torches in their Nuptiall solemnities. Whether there were any mystery or not implied, the most generative animals were created on this day, and had accordingly the largest benediction: And under a Quintuple consideration, wanton Antiquity considered the Circumstances of generation, while by this number of five they naturally divided the Nectar of the fifth Planet.

The same number in the Hebrew mysteries and Cabalistical accounts was the character of Generation; declared by the Letter *He*, the fifth in their Alphabet; According to that Cabalisticall *Dogma*: If *Abram* had not had this Letter added unto his Name he had remained fruitlesse, and without the power of generation: Not onely because hereby the number of his Name attained two hundred fourty eight, the number of the affirmative precepts, but because as in created natures there is a male and female, so in divine and intelligent productions, the mother of Life and Fountain of souls in Cabalisticall Technology is called *Binah*; whose Seal and Character was *He*. So that being sterill before, he received the power of generation from that measure and mansion in the Archetype; and was made conformable unto *Binah*. And upon such involved considerations, the ten of *Sarai* was exchanged into five. If any shall look upon this as a stable number, and fitly appropriable unto Trees, as Bodies of Rest and Station, he hath herein a great Foundation in nature, who observing much variety in legges and motive Organs of Animals, as two, four, six, eight, twelve, fourteen, and more, hath passed over five and ten, and assigned them unto none. And for the stability of this Number, he shall not want the sphericity of its nature, which multiplied in it self, will return into its own denomination, and bring up the reare of the account. Which is also one of the Numbers that makes up the mysticall Name of God, which consisting of Letters denoting all the sphæricall Numbers, ten, five, and six; Emphatically sets forth the Notion of *Trismegistus*, and that intelligible Sphere which is the Nature of God.

Many Expressions by this Number occurre in Holy Scripture, perhaps unjustly laden with mysticall Expositions, and little concerning our order. That the Israelites were forbidden to eat the fruit of their new planted Trees before the fifth yeare, was very agreeable unto the naturall Rules of Husbandry: Fruits being unwholsome and lash before the fourth or fifth Yeare. In the second day or Feminine part of five, there was added no approbation. For in the third or masculine day, the same is twice repeated; and a double benediction inclosed both Creations, whereof the one in some part was but an accomplishment of the other. That the Trespasser was to pay a fifth part above the head or principall, makes no secret in this Number, and implied no more than one part above the principall; which being considered in four parts, the additionall forfeit must bear the Name of a fift. The five golden mice had plainly their determination from the number of the Princes; That five should put to flight an hundred might have nothing mystically implyed; considering a rank of Souldiers could scarce consist of a lesser number. Saint *Paul* had rather speak five words in a known than ten thousand in an unknowne tongue: That is as little as could well be spoken. A simple proposition consisting of three words and a complexed one not ordinarily short of five.

More considerable there are in this mysticall account, which we must not insist on. And therefore why the radicall Letters in the Pentateuch should equall the number of the Souldiery of the Tribes; Why our Saviour in the Wildernesse fed five thousand persons with five Barley Loaves, and again but four thousand with no lesse than seven of Wheat? Why *Joseph* designed five changes of Rayment unto *Benjamin*? and *David* took just five pibbles out of the Brook against the Pagan Champion? We leave it unto Arithmeticall Divinity, and Theologicall explanation.

Yet if any delight in new Problemes, or think it worth the enquiry, whether the Criticall Physician hath rightly hit the nominall notation of Quinque; Why the Ancients mixed five or three but not four parts of water unto their Wine: And *Hippocrates* observed a fifth proportion in the mixture of water with milk, as in *Dysenteries* and bloudy fluxes. Under what abstruse foundation Astrologers do Figure the good

or bad Fate from our Children, in good Fortune, or
the fifth house of their Celestiall Schemes. Whether the
Ægyptians described a Starr by a Figure of five points,
with reference unto the five Capitall aspects, whereby they
transmit their Influences, or abstruser Considerations? Why
the Cabalisticall Doctors, who conceive the whole *Sephiroth*
or divine emanations to have guided the ten-stringed Harp
of *David*, whereby he pacified the evil spirit of *Saul*, in
strict numeration doe begin with the Perihypate Meson,
or si fa ut, and so place the Tiphereth answering C sol
fa ut, upon the fifth string: Or whether this number be
oftner applied unto bad things and ends than good in holy
Scripture, and why? He may meet with abstrusities of no ready
resolution.

If any shall question the rationality of that Magick, in the
cure of the blind man by *Serapis*, commanded to place five
fingers on his Altar, and then his hand on his Eyes? Why
since the whole Comœdy is primarily and naturally comprised
in four parts, and Antiquity permitted not so many persons
to speak in one Scene, yet would not comprehend the same
in more or lesse than five acts? Why amongst Sea-starres
nature chiefly delighteth in five points? And since there are
found some of no fewer than twelve, and some of seven, and
nine, there are few or none discovered of six or eight? If any
shall enquire why the Flowers of *Rue* properly consisting of
four Leaves, The first and third Flower have five? Why since
many Flowers have one leaf or none, as *Scaliger* will have it,
diverse three, and the greatest number consist of five divided
from their bottomes; there are yet so few of two: or why
nature generally beginning or setting out with two opposite
leaves at the Root, doth so seldome conclude with that order
and number at the Flower? he shall not passe his hours in
vulgar speculations.

If any shall further quæry why magneticall Philosophy
excludeth decussations, and needles transversly placed do
naturally distract their verticities? Why Geomancers do
imitate the Quintuple Figure, in their Mother Characters of
Acquisition and Amission, &c. somewhat answering the
Figures in the Lady or speckled Beetle? With what Equity,
Chiromanticall conjecturers decry these decussations in the
Lines and Mounts of the hand? What that decussated Figure
intendeth in the medall of *Alexander* the Great? Why the
Goddesses sit commonly crosse-legged in ancient draughts,
Since *Juno* is described in the same as a veneficial posture to
hinder the birth of *Hercules*? If any shall doubt why at the
Amphidromicall Feasts, on the fifth day after the Childe was
born presents were sent from friends, of *Polipusses*, and
Cuttle-fishes? Why five must be only left in that Symbolicall
mutiny among the men of *Cadmus*? Why *Proteus* in *Homer*
the Symbole of the first matter, before he setled himself in the
midst of his Sea-monsters, doth place them out by fives?
Why the fifth years Oxe was acceptable Sacrifice unto *Jupiter*?
Or why the Noble *Antoninus* in some sence doth call the soul
it self a Rhombus? He shall not fall on trite or triviall dis-
quisitions. And these we invent and propose unto acuter
enquirers, nauseating crambe verities and questions over-
queried. Flat and flexible truths are beat out by every hammer;
But *Vulcan* and his whole forge sweat to work out *Achilles*
his armour. A large field is yet left unto sharper discerners to
enlarge upon this order, to search out the *quaternio's* and
figured draughts of this nature, and moderating the study of
names, and meer nomenclature of plants, to erect generalities,
disclose unobserved proprieties, not only in the vegetable
shop, but the whole volume of nature; affording delightful
Truths, confirmable by sense and ocular Observation, which
seems to me the surest path, to trace the Labyrinth of Truth.

For though discursive enquiry and rationall conjecture may leave handsome gashes and flesh-wounds; yet without conjunction of this, expect no mortal or dispatching blows unto errour.

But the Quincunx of Heaven runs low, and 'tis time to close the five ports of knowledge; We are unwilling to spin out our awaking thoughts into the phantasmes of sleep, which too often continueth præcogitations; making Cables of Cobwebbes and Wildernesses of handsome Groves. Beside, *Hippocrates* hath spoke so little, and the Oneirocriticall Masters have left such frigid Interpretations from plants, that there is little encouragement to dream of Paradise it self. Nor will the sweetest delight of Gardens afford much comfort in sleep; wherein the dulnesse of that sense shakes hands with delectable odours; and though in the Bed of *Cleopatra*, can hardly with any delight raise up the ghost of a Rose.

Night which Pagan Theology could make the daughter of *Chaos*, affords no advantage to the description of order: Although no lower than that Masse can we derive its Genealogy. All things began in order, so shall they end, and so shall they begin again; according to the ordainer of order and mysticall Mathematicks of the City of Heaven.

Though *Somnus* in *Homer* be sent to rowse up *Agamemnon*, I finde no such effects in the drowsy approaches of sleep. To keep our eyes open longer were but to act our *Antipodes*. The Huntsmen are up in *America*, and they are already past their first sleep in *Persia*. But who can be drowsie at that howr which freed us from everlasting sleep? or have slumbring thoughts at that time, when sleep it self must end, and as some conjecture all shall awake again?

FINIS

AUTHOR-CORRECTED COPIES OF THE FIRST EDITION, 1658

IN 1930, when Mr Desmond Flower invited me to attempt a fresh recension of *Urne Buriall and The Garden of Cyrus*, six copies of the original edition were known to me with textual and marginal corrections in the author's hand. These were described in an appendix to Messrs Cassell's edition published, with a series of noble designs by Paul Nash, in 1932, and their readings, as incorporated into its text, were noted in the *apparatus criticus*. Some of those in the copy in the library of Trinity College, Cambridge, had been used by Charles Sayle in his edition of 1904, and those in the Osler copy (McGill University, Montreal) by Sir Geoffrey Keynes in 1929.

Since 1932 six further author-corrected copies have been found and their particulars published: by Dr Jeremiah Finch of Princeton in the *Times Literary Supplement*, 16 March 1940, and in *The Library*, vol. XIX (1938), p. 347; and by myself in *T.L.S.* 22 August 1935, 27 February 1943, 30 August 1957, and in *The Library*, 5th series, vol. II (1947), p. 191. Such additional contributions as these copies afford to a more accurate text have been incorporated in the present edition.

The author-corrected copies now known (others may still lurk undetected) are as follows, with the number of autograph corrections, as identified to the best of my ability.*

1 Avery Library, Columbia University, New York—77
2 Osler Library, McGill University, Montreal—49
3 Reynolds Library, University of Alabama—45
4 Trinity College, Cambridge—44
5 John Carter, London—43
6 Durham University Library—42

* I have examined them all except no. 12, for which I have depended on photographs.

7 British Museum—40
8 Princeton University Library—39
9 The late Dr Eli Moschcowitz—29
10 Lilly Library, Indiana University (previously Beyer)—17
11 Yale University Library—16
12 Cornell University Library—3

Several of these copies were originally gifts from the author, in which it may legitimately be presumed that he made, before despatching them, some at least of the corrections necessitated by the imperfect printing of the first edition. Of the others it can only be hazarded that when Sir Thomas found a copy on a friend's table, he did the same.

Many of the corrections thus made were indicated in the errata (first of eighteen lines, subsequently of twenty-four lines) which are found in a minority of copies of the first edition, or in the longer list normally accompanying copies of the second (4to 1658). But in most of the author-corrected copies, which seem to have been annotated in a very haphazard fashion, there are some corrections independent of any of the printed errata; and while most of these in each copy are supported by the same corrections in another, in a few cases the correction depends for its authority on Sir Thomas's hand at this one point only.

In a good many surviving copies of the first edition (including several of those with Browne's own corrections), some early owner's pen has transferred to text or margin corrections from the printed errata; so that manuscript marginalia need to be carefully scrutinised. In three copies known to me (Moschcowitz, hand B, the Wilkin copy at Norwich, and the copy in the library of the University of Adelaide, particulars of which I owe to the kindness of Professor R. C. Bald) there is reason to suppose that certain early corrections independent of the printed errata, though not in Browne's hand, must derive from a copy corrected by him.

A NOTE ON THE TEXT

THE present text is based, with the courteous permission of Messrs Cassell, on that constructed for their edition of 1932. That was itself based on the first edition. Every departure from this (except for such purely typographical errors as turned, dropped or transposed letters) was noted in the *apparatus criticus* to the Cassell edition, which was too elaborate to repeat in a reading edition and to which readers concerned with such things are referred.

The text of the present *editio minor* differs from my earlier recension in three respects only. It incorporates a handful of readings gleaned from subsequently discovered copies of the first edition corrected by the author (see Appendix A), with the Avery copy the most considerable contributor. These and a few other emendations, other than of punctuation, are set out below.

Then, a quarter of a century's reflection has convinced me of the over-severity of my earlier reaction against the indiscriminate re-punctuating, modernisation of spelling, romanising of italics, demotion of initial capitals and the like, which characterised most of my editorial predecessors. Sir Thomas Browne's use of commas and semicolons, like his use of initial capitals and italics, is too characteristic to submit to any wholesale streamlining. But there are some seventeenth-century usages which are confusing, if not actively misleading, today: such as the optional spellings of *of* for *off*, *set* for *sit*, *then* for *than*, *humane* for *human*, *whether* for *whither*; the long *s*; and the habit, obsolescent and capricious by 1658, of printing *U* as *V*.

There are also passages where random punctuation, which one prefers, however doubtfully, to attribute to the press-corrector rather than to the author, positively obscures the sense. I have made the few such adjustments as seemed to me necessary for the reader's understanding, without feeling an obligation to list every one of them: taking as my guiding principle a paragraph in the preface to Capel Lofft's edition of *Paradise Lost* (Bury St Edmund's,

1792): 'I mean, that it should be a likeness of the revered original in every permanent, expressive, characteristic feature; but not in every freckle, scar, or casual blemish.'

Thirdly, the notes printed in the margins of the original and in most subsequent editions (including my own of 1932) are almost all references, usually in abbreviated, often in almost shorthand, form. Since this edition is designed for the general reader, not for the antiquarian or for the specialist, they have been omitted.

Sir Thomas Browne has been fortunate in his editors. To omit the living, his readers have reason (and none better reason than myself) to be grateful for the scholarly care of Simon Wilkin (1836), of W. A. Greenhill (1896), and of W. Murison (1922), whose edition in the Pitt Press series, still happily in print, provides the most sensible annotation available for these two highly alembicated essays.

EMENDATION IN THE PRESENT TEXT
(1932 READINGS FIRST)

P. 8, l. 3   *a mixture* * *admixture*   Author's correction in the Avery copy.

P. 48, l. 4   *contriving* * *continuing*   This emendation, noted but not adopted in my earlier text, was suggested by Mr John Sparrow. The compositor seems to have had difficulty in distinguishing between these two words in Browne's script: cf. a confusion in the opposite direction at p. 27, l. 10, where the first edition's *continued upon Tiberius* was corrected to *contrived* by the early hand in the Moschcowitz copy (a good secondary authority) and in the editions of St John, 1838, Bayne, 1906, and Keynes, 1929, all judicious editors. Cf. also a confusion between the same two words in Hooker's *Lawes of Ecclesiastical Politie*, cited by Percy Simpson, *Proof Reading*, p. 79.

P. 48, l. 30   *who can only* * *who only can*

P. 49, ll. 25–27   I have reverted to the punctuation of the first edition.

P. 60, l. 18   *transverly* * *transversely*.

P. 62, l. 17   *Eustachius* * *Eustathius*   Author's correction in the Reynolds copy.

P. 67, l. 6   *chapters* * *chapiters*   Author's correction in the Avery, Osler and Princeton copies (also errata to second edition and several later editors, but overlooked by me in 1932).

P. 67, l. 30   *pictures* * *picturers*   Author's correction in the Avery copy.

P. 68, l. 28   The full point after *Squares* in the 1932 text was a misprint for the first edition's comma.

P. 68, l. 29   *Chet mat*   This word is not in O.E.D., but Dr Finch identifies it with the Persian chess term *shah mat*, meaning 'the King is dead' (i.e. 'check mate', which is the emendation of the fourth edition, 1669).

P. 68, l. 30   *continue*   After some doubts I have retained this, the reading of the first and all later editions, assuming that it is used in the well-authenticated contemporary sense of 'contain'.

P. 69, l. 6   *division* * *divisions*   Author's correction in the Durham copy.

P. 70, l. 20   *fixt pike* * *sixt[h] pike*   Second and most later editions: faulty impression in the first edition makes the initial long *s* look like an *f* in all copies I have lately seen.

P. 73, l. 17   *head of Taurus*   I have retained this reading (the first and other early editions read *neck*), since the already-cited authority of the author's corrections in my own and the Yale copy and of the errata to the second edition (followed by Wilkin, Greenhill and Keynes) is now further buttressed by the author's corrections in the Avery, British Museum, Princeton and Reynolds copies and the revised issue of the errata to the first edition (first publicly noted in 1947). But it must be recorded that in the Cornell copy Browne corrected *neck* to *front*, and that the correction is also made in this form both by the early hand in the Wilkin copy, whose several verified corrections independent of the errata imply an author-corrected exemplar, and in the Moschcowitz copy either by (as I think) that early hand which may claim the same sort of authority or (as Dr Finch thinks) by the author. Where the

Doctor disagrees with himself, his editor is in a quandary. But *head* has more of his authority than *front* on present evidence.

P. 74, l. 3   *Tapsas* * *Tapsus*   Author's correction in the Avery copy, confirming the reading of the second and other editions.

P. 94, l. 18   *generality* * *generallitie*   Despite the errata to the second edition the author's corrections (from the first edition's *generation*) in the Avery and British Museum copies suggest that this was his preferred spelling.

P. 96, l. 21   *placed inwardly against a South-window* * *placed inwardly in a chamber against a South-window*   Author's insertion in the Avery copy, confirming the same insertion made by the early hands in the Moschcowitz and Adelaide copies.

P. 114, l. 7   *which often* * *which to[o] often*   Author's correction in the Avery copy.

(It is a satisfaction so seldom vouchsafed to an editor to have his emendations subsequently confirmed by a long-dead author that I cannot resist recording that, of the very few which I ventured on my own responsibility in 1932, the Avery copy now establishes *inter-arborations* at p. 102, l. 19 and *consisting* at p. 112, l. 25.)

19697750R00078

Printed in Great Britain
by Amazon